MANUAL
FOR LIVING

A USER'S GUIDE TO THE MEANING OF LIFE

REALITY

Highlights

- Happiness can be momentary, but true and sustainable happiness requires fulfillment of our being, of our soul.

- We all seem to have the answers for everyone else's life, but rarely for our own.

- We tread through our lives believing that we never have enough, where we are is not where we should be, and who we are is not good enough.

- Everything that happens to us happens within us.

- When life is most difficult, our need to trust is foremost.

- It may take time, but in due course, we will discover and understand the meaning in all things.

- We are constantly tested and pressed hard for growth, yet we must create the space for greatness in every moment.

- Focusing on someone else's life is a poor excuse for disregarding our own.

- A life without meaning is no life at all.

- True happiness, peace, fulfillment, and success are found in the current moment, irrespective of the past or future.

- It is our ability to adapt efficiently and effectively to obstacles as they are presented that determines the extent to which we evolve or the degree to which we suffer.

- Step away from normalcy and become unpredictable; move from complacency to greatness; transcend mediocrity into excellence.

- The greatness we seek in the world needs to be mirrored not only by that which we seek within ourselves, but also by the manner and method in which we live our lives.

- Sometimes being human is extremely painful, especially when we don't listen to our truth, we ignore our path and purpose, and we disregard our calling in life.

- We must listen to our heart and our soul, for we are not always given the guidance we desire, but the guidance we require.

- By looking at someone else's problems, we temporarily lose sight of our own, and comparatively the challenges of our life don't seem quite as momentous.

- Our reality is what we perceive it to be.

- There is nothing we can digest, absorb, inhale, ingest, or inject that can fulfill, supplement, or replace our path in life.

- Our body is not designed to last forever—that is the role of our soul.

- In every moment, we are either living or dying; there is nothing in between.

- We cannot avoid death, but somehow we have discovered how to avoid life.

- The only path to happiness is a life of purpose and meaning.

- There is never enough money for all that we desire, but there are ample funds for all that we require.

- Happiness, fulfillment, and connection are the true prosperity of the soul.

MANUAL
FOR LIVING

A USER'S GUIDE TO THE MEANING OF LIFE

REALITY

SETH DAVID CHERNOFF

SPIRIT SCOPE
PUBLISHING

Spirit Scope Publishing
6525 Gunpark Drive, Suite 370-249
Boulder, CO 80301
www.SpiritScope.com
Books@SpiritScope.com

Library of Congress Cataloging-in-Publication Data
Chernoff, Seth David, 1975–
    Manual for Living: Reality, a User's Guide to the Meaning of Life / by Seth David Chernoff
    p. cm.
    ISBN: 978-0-9840930-9-0
    1. Spirituality 2. Mind, Body & Spirit I. Title

Library of Congress Control Number: 2010904786

First Edition, June 2010

If you are unable to order this book from your local bookseller, you may order directly from the publisher. Copies are available at special rates for bulk orders. Contact the publisher at www.SpiritScope.com or Books@SpiritScope.com.

Author Website: www.SethChernoff.com
Book Website: www.ManualForLiving.com

For Mat
Be of service & never let go of your dreams.

Dedicated to my queen,
our beautiful boys,
my parents, my brother,
and you.

Contents

Prologue

———◆◆———

L IKE MANY, AS A CHILD I WAS GIFTED WITH NUMEROUS
insights and understandings, yet I spent decades ignoring my
inner wisdom and truth, only to stumble and fall over and over again,
as much the result of inner turmoil as external mayhem. I have been
challenged spiritually, intellectually, emotionally and physically; when
I clearly could handle no more, the havoc and opportunity only grew
larger. Sometimes I allowed myself to become engulfed by extreme
pain and suffering, but only in direct proportion to my own ignorance
and disregard for my truth and path in life.

In the end, my life has been exhilarating and spectacular in many ways,
with every experience granting me the opportunity to grow, to learn,
and to evolve. I have survived cancer on two separate occasions, lived
with chronic headaches every single day of my life since I was five-years-
old, and experienced extreme physical pain so unbearable that I became
physically sick and temporarily paralyzed. As traumatic as the physical
pain was, it paled in comparison to the mental, emotional and spiritual
growth I was afforded through this and countless other opportunities.

⊱ Through hardship came strength, and as a result of pain I
found joy. Through suffering came gratitude, and by letting
go I found my path and purpose in life.

I have experienced the fullness of so much of life—the magnificence and the betrayal, true happiness and heartbreaking sadness, sickness and health, life and death, and true love. I have searched everywhere for the answers, but eventually realized that the guidance I desired was actually here for me all along, not from outside myself, but from within. It was then that I found my truth and my purpose in life.

We each have a distinct path and purpose in life, a destiny as unique as our own fingerprints or DNA structure, yet we often live lives of petty obscurity and quiet desperation, ignoring our truth and our path, choosing to blame others instead of taking responsibility for our own choices. Instead of receiving true happiness, love, and fulfillment, we experience it through a commitment to serve others and to find excellence in life. What if you really were in control of your life? What if you accepted that your current state of affairs was entirely the result of the choices you've made and the actions you've taken? What if you acknowledged that the present condition of your home, the quality of your relationships, your fulfillment at work, the size of your bank account, and the level of happiness you felt inside were 100% the result of all of the decisions you've made throughout your entire life? What if you stopped giving away your power and instead invested your time and energy into the creation of your life in exactly the form and manner you desired?

⸜ What if this book could help you find happiness, fulfillment, and love?

In life we often are forced to learn our lessons the hard way; through trial and tribulation, pain and suffering, failure and defeat. What if it didn't have to be that way? What if we could learn through others, by listening to the knowledge and wisdom of those who have travelled the road before us? What if we listened to our own truth and followed our inner guidance? We can alter and advance our consciousness in respect to all that we believe to be true. Take advantage of this information as it is the culmination of a life lived through growth, dedication, and purpose.

> ⤳ If you resist reading what you disagree with, how will you ever acquire deeper insights into what you believe? The things most worth reading are precisely those that challenge our convictions.
> —Author Unknown

A healthy skepticism is crucial to navigating the life-path before us and eventually discovering our truth and finding our inner voice. I ask you simply to try this on, take it as your own: Give your life a chance to become everything you choose it to be, everything you imagine it to be. Every chapter in this book has the possibility of enhancing your life, improving your relationships, deepening your understanding, and bringing you closer to true happiness and fulfillment.

> ⤳ Don't expect that someone else will step in to fulfill the purpose you neglect, the path you disregard. Life is far too short, and your life is far too important.

Don't sacrifice your truth or your values, for we each have our special place within this world, and it is our prerogative to find that purpose and fulfill it with every morsel of our being. The loss of a life is not nearly as devastating as the loss of what could have been, of the dreams left unfulfilled and lingering passions undiscovered. This is not a book about religion; it is a book about life for those who choose to grow, who desire a more fulfilled life, and who accept that we are only as magnificent as we choose to be in this moment. This book is a reflection of my personal path in life, and I hope you will find it useful as you navigate your own.

Introduction

> ~ How do we fully engage with that which lies dormant within us?
>
> ~ What are we afraid to lose?

THE *MANUAL FOR LIVING* IS A USER'S GUIDE TO THE MEANING of life; it is a guidebook to balance and connection, intimacy and relationship, peace and love, evolution and fulfillment. What we desire cannot be "obtained," for it can only be experienced—the result of a life of commitment and service. Can we achieve lasting happiness? Can we find fulfillment or obtain true love? What exactly is a spiritual life, an inspirational life, a fulfilled life? What really is possible in life? Can we have it all?

The *Manual* will help you find clarity and assist you with connecting to your inner guidance—thus opening the gateway to an intentional life—a chosen life that is joyful and fulfilled. Few people on Earth possess the answers to life's simplest questions because in truth, answers are granted only to those with literacy in a language all their own.

~ In life, answers often result only in further inquiry; the meaning we seek is found in the journey itself.

Inquiry and curiosity become the lifeblood of the living—the keys to assist us in our personal journey. We stay the course, learning through our environment and life experiences, challenges and opportunities. An individual's inquiry may actually safeguard against the very answers he or she seeks; the questions themselves being an indicator of the quasi-destination. We journey through the spiral of human evolution toward an existence of contemplation, verbalization, connection, contribution, service, fulfillment, and happiness.

The answer to life's meaning is different for every one of us and dwells somewhere deep within the epicenter of our being. We are in control of our heart, mind, and soul, and therein resides the core truth of existence. In large part, we are all identical, sharing similar core needs, wants, and desires. Inevitably, we will struggle with the same core issues and challenges. The greatest commonality of all humanity is that of life itself and its finality.

The *Manual's* purpose is to help you find true happiness, understand why you are here, and discover your true purpose in life. Challenge your beliefs and assumptions, and find your inner voice and truth in the process. Create the life you've always wanted by overcoming the obstacles before you, finding courage in the face of fear or adversity. Find the joy and magnificence in all things, and discover a new level of gratitude for everything that you have been given. Learn how to be fully in the moment and to let go of everything that stands in your way. Ease your pain, suffering, and struggle while embracing and overcoming the lessons before you. Encounter true balance, eternal happiness, and a powerful connection to your source. Learn to coexist and to function successfully on this physical plane without sacrificing your spiritual core. Find true happiness on your path, and achieve everything you believe is possible.

The *Manual* is a practical guide to the hidden truths in life, basic pearls of insight to guide your way along life's path. It will help you better understand the role we all play as physical and spiritual beings of service to the greater good of humankind. Along the way, you may discover the meaning behind your own eternal search. The *Manual* will help you to amplify your spiritual journey of enthusiastic selflessness and pride in giving, allowing you to better focus your attention and manifest your reality through continuous evolution.

➤ We all have much in common, yet we often feel so distant from one another.

In truth, we are all one in the same, regardless of intellect, age, race, creed, or dialect. No matter how much we contest this truth, there is little difference between us except how we have chosen to experience this lifetime. Life seems easier when we live as turtles, hiding in the shadows and emerging to seek nourishment, prosperity, and fulfillment, only to retreat into the protection of our shell when we realize that what we seek cannot be found outside of ourselves. Seldom are rewards granted to those who hide from the world and its associated challenges and opportunities.

➤ Opportunities are endless when we choose to take risks and become present in our life.

This *Manual* is here to assist you in understanding and choosing a life fulfilled over a life of mediocrity, desperation, pettiness, or even worse, no life at all. When life is amazing, fulfilling, and spectacular, this *Manual* may gather dust; however, when you are faced with hurdles, challenges, and pain, it may help you persevere and be of service to those who await your guidance. The *Manual for Living* is a guide to support all beings in truth; to help us turn toward courage, honesty, integrity, and love; and to make conscious decisions that will ultimately guide us to true happiness and fulfillment.

⊱ Whether our path is direct or circuitous, our destinations are constant; the eternal continuance of time combines with the temporal aspect of our physical existence.

———————⊷ ⊶———————

Note to Reader

———◆◆———

FOR THE SAKE OF CLARITY, I HAVE CHOSEN TO USE TERMS such as "Higher Consciousness" and "Spirit" within the pages of this book to describe the one all-encompassing entity, the guiding power within us all. The spiritual being within and around each of us is the energy to which we grant so many names and even greater responsibility.

Please note that this book is not designed to be read from cover to cover. In fact, you may find it most useful reading it one section at a time. When you require guidance, simply choose a chapter from the table of contents or take a full breath and randomly open the book. You may find yourself pleasantly surprised by the relevancy of the information you discover. Some of this information might be obscure or multifaceted, so take your time and give your mind, heart, and soul the opportunity to process what is being shared.

Enjoy!

———◆◆———

Time

Where are we going, and why?

What's the rush?

Why are we unable to be fully present in the moment before us?

Time Enough for Everything

A person often meets his destiny on the road he took to avoid it.
—Jean de La Fontaine

> ~ Why are we all in such a hurry? Where are we going?
>
> ~ How many physical ailments and diseases are self-inflicted, caused by frustration, anxiety, or stress?
>
> ~ How many accidents are a result of distraction, fretfulness, and pre-occupation?

TODAY, WE LIVE LONGER THAN GENERATIONS PAST, BUT WE are still dying too early in life—not necessarily physically, but emotionally, mentally, and spiritually. In fact, for every moment that we don't consciously choose life, we subsequently choose death, for we are in perpetual motion; life never stops. We are subject to extreme external pressures in this life, and we must focus on only those things that we are able to control. But that which we can control, we generally control inadequately.

~ We tread through our lives believing that we never have enough, where we are is not where we should be, and who we are is not good enough.

We are taught that society awards perfection, and those of us who merely scrape by are less valuable or less important than those who excel. We are taught that in order to be great, we have to do better, be more, achieve more, and have more. As a result, throughout life we actually *become* less and less. We don't evolve; we merely become distracted and preoccupied. We have more things, but less time. We have a bigger house, but less of a connection with our loved ones. We have success in our material world, yet we are empty inside.

We must slow down, take care of ourselves, and take better care of those around us. We must make decisions that are in alignment with our core values and our inner truth. We need to seize life in this moment and fully accept that suffering and unhappiness are self-inflicted, for they are inner responses to external circumstances. Many diseases are caused by anxiety, and many accidents are caused by ignorance. By appreciating the pleasures of the moment, not only will we live more fulfilled lives, but also lives full of quality, connection, and growth. Every day we must simply rise and do our best regardless of the time allotted, for the dawn of a new day will come and with luck, we will have the opportunity to begin all over again.

~ Every moment grants us the opportunity to choose life, even as the alternative is inevitable.

Universal Time

The cyclone derives its powers from a calm center.
So does a person.
—Norman Vincent Peale

- ᕈ Why do we attempt to govern every aspect of our existence around the presence of time?

- ᕈ Can we really micromanage our life according to a plan?

- ᕈ When is the schedule of the universe in alignment with our own?

- ᕈ Does spirituality have a "time" associated with it?

- ᕈ Why do we even believe in a time continuum?

TIME EXISTS AND OPERATES ONLY AS A FUNCTION OF OUR OWN belief system. We have a schedule, yet our perception of control is governed by a higher schedule, that of the universe itself or that of our soul. We live on our own time, yet we are governed by the timeline of the universe. We have certain deadlines and commitments to meet, but beyond all of our structure, we run on our *soul's* clock, on *universal time*.

⁊ We cannot rush the path of life, for we are at the beck and call of the life-path we have chosen.

The linear aspects of life are only perceptions assumed by humankind and are likely not shared by all within this universe. We generally believe that the time continuum consists of equal segments of action and inaction that are partitioned into the past, present, and future. Our world is simply the combination of all the individual moments within it, within each moment dissected into varying segments of time. In reality, there is no direct correlation between each moment and our attempt to quantify them into hours, minutes, and seconds. Time is a variable created by humankind as an attempt to quantify and qualify that which cannot be controlled.

⁊ Time is the representation of our feeble attempts to calculate, track, and quantify our existence.

Of course there is a time continuum, one that we created for our own piece of mind in an attempt to understand the larger transgressions of the universe and our life within it. Frustration often occurs in life when we attempt to control that which cannot be controlled. For example, our meager attempts to have power over time itself, to control our environment, or to influence other human beings, often results only in disappointment.

⁊ We must accept that which we cannot control; our feeble attempts to the contrary generally end with our own pain and suffering.

Our inner spirit requires very little for its own health and happiness, and by releasing others from the schedule we attempt to keep, we have the opportunity to find the moment-by-moment happiness in all that we desire. Time exists as a function of the experiences we share in every moment throughout the course of our existence. We can label those very experiences however we desire, but it is the joy and love we share in every moment that determines the level of fulfillment and happiness we experience, having no correlation whatsoever to the actual *amount* of time involved.

Death is inevitable whether by choice or by default. By letting go of our own attachment to the rigidity of time, we have much more of it to appreciate by being present to the magnificence of the present moment before us. Sometimes we must simply go with the flow and allow the transgressions of our world to guide us along our individual paths. Time often serves to limit our focus on the moment instead of being present to it, for integrating structure over freedom, although boundaries are often a necessary evil, quite often diminishes our experience of life.

~ Eventually we must fully release our own agenda for what the universe has in store for us.

Past & Present

———◆◆———

Anyone who keeps the ability to see beauty never grows old.
—Kafka

⤳ Why are we stuck in the past?

⤳ Why is it such a challenge to maintain our inner peace?

⤳ Why do we fixate on and obsess about the future?

OUR REACTION TO A SPECIFIC SITUATION IS DEPENDENT upon a combination of who we are or we choose to be in the moment, our past experiences, karmic impulses, current reality, the potential impact on our life, among a multitude of other elements. As a result, given the exact same situation, all parties may experience it, react to it, and recollect it differently, thereby making it almost impossible for any sort of consensus or agreement to be reached. Predicting the future is hard enough, but predicting individual behavior or the reaction of another given an inevitable outcome is impossible.

∼ As living and breathing organisms, each of us has a unique role in this existence, and our reactions are as vast as our individuality.

Life is an ever-evolving process of understanding the current moment and then recreating it with an entirely new understanding, for it continually evolves as do each of us. We find a moment of peace and suddenly the moment to follow is unpredictable and unexpected as we are faced with another opportunity for growth. The toolbox of the soul contains more subtleties than our imagination can even begin to comprehend. We are presented in every moment with an opportunity for greatness or an opportunity for growth. Moments continually evolve because they are a reflection of our relationship to them and the society in which we live, and we simultaneously adapt and evolve to handle better what we are presented with.

∼ Completely releasing the past is the only way to fully appreciate and accept the opportunities before us.

We must open our minds to what is possible within the moment rather than to what might be possible in the future or what dwells in our reflections of the past. True evolution and growth comes from appreciation of not only what is, but also what is truly available to us at any instant. As individuals within a community that holds to a communal vision, the collective power of moment-by-moment gratitude, fulfillment, and opportunity distinguishes us from those who pray for a resurrection of the past at some point in the future.

∼ Waiting for the future or attempting to relive the past inherently disregards the magnificence of what is available in and around us in every breath and in every passing moment.

Time & Dreams

The obstacle is the path.
—Zen Proverb

➤ Why doesn't hard work always equate with results or fulfillment?

➤ Why can't we evolve through effort alone?

➤ Why does receiving everything we desire not guarantee happiness?

WE ARE TAUGHT TO BELIEVE THAT THROUGH HARD WORK, we can achieve any goal, any dream. However, we are not taught that by obsessing about our work, we can isolate ourselves from our friends, our families, and most importantly, distance ourselves from our path and purpose in life for the potential fulfillment of an empty dream or an idealistic goal. We seldom realize that the very goals we desire are often in direct contrast to our inner truth, our reason for living, and our purpose in life. We rarely understand that who we are, where we are going, and our ability to create can be in direct contrast with that which we inherently desire.

⤳ The trite needs of this physical existence rarely, if ever, fulfill our soul's desire for sustenance.

A conscious life requires hard and diligent effort, and we must continuously re-evaluate our assumptions in order to ensure that what we think we will obtain is in accordance with what we manifest in our lives. Hard work, in and of itself, will bring us no closer to our goal than mere focused thought, but focused and intentional effort will bring us everything we require. Our excess exertion often prevents us from seeing the truth and from seeing the possibility that we might be headed in the wrong direction. We are frequently blind to the fact that we have been guided to a specific destination, and often our personal and professional goals, and physical and tangible desires do not align with that destination.

⤳ Through peace we find connection, and through connection we are presented with the answers we seek.

Presently, humans can run faster than at any time in recorded history, but if we travel in the wrong direction, our speed has no relevance. We are better off traveling slowly and with intention, heeding the guidance we are given, to ensure that we continue in the right direction. Through intention we travel with only spiritual wind giving our wings the needed lift, achieving more than we ever will through hard work, dedication, and effort alone. We are unable to fathom with our conscious intellect the deep interconnectedness of our greater spiritual society. As a result, while we are given the opportunity to primarily trust ourselves and our inner truth, we are also guided by those people and events that occur along our periphery of understanding and awareness, a place we may not fully comprehend or even trust to exist. Trusting is one of life's greatest challenges, for in times of greatest need, it is what we question first and foremost.

⤳ When life is most difficult, our need to trust is foremost.

We live in a moment-to-moment reality, storing relics of the past while being forced to trust in the future. Trust is all we have; our control of the present often has little or no relation to the future. It is difficult to control what we cannot see, what we cannot touch, and what we cannot feel, but life is not limited to our physical senses. As a society, we are pushed to believe either in destiny's predetermination or the obscure alternative of taking responsibility for the aspects of life that are within our control, and often mistakenly attempting to control everything else.

In destiny, we have the opportunity to blame and take no responsibility for the situations and experiences we find ourselves in, yet as with all of life, there is balance in all things. We balance a certain predetermination with a level of responsibility. We take responsibility for that which we can control and relinquish that which we cannot. It is through this balance that we create a partnership with our higher selves and are able to co-create our world. We live in partnership; we take responsibility, and we trust in what the future will bring, for as individuals and as a society, we are destined for greatness.

⤳ We have the opportunity, but not the obligation, to experience aspects of life effortlessly when we listen to our own truth and consciously follow it.

Timelessness & Understanding

*There is nothing like returning to a place that remains unchanged
to find the ways in which you yourself have altered.*
—Nelson Mandela

> ~ Why does time appear to move slowly at certain times and
> faster at others?
>
> ~ Why does it seem that time moves slower when we're young,
> increasing in speed as we age?
>
> ~ Why does time seem to move faster when we are joyful and
> happy and more slowly when we are miserable?

SINCE TIME DOES NOT REALLY EXIST OUTSIDE OF THIS TEMPO-
ral reality, all aspects of our lives and the experiences in and around
it are merely factors of the present moment. As human beings, we
have the ability to create our life on a moment-by-moment basis in
the unique manner and method we see fit, albeit within the structure
and reality that we set forth. The prospect of the future, or the future

present as it can be called, is available to all of us with both its greatness and its challenges.

⟜ Without any interference, we will move through life in exactly the direction we are headed, for our destination is a direct function of our current position and the choices we make in every moment.

With enhanced levels of awareness, we may move through life quickly, or in rebellion we may move through slowly, but we are in perpetual motion and our final destinations are equal. The eternal lifeline of our soul incorporates all that we are able to absorb and comprehend for all of eternity, directly and continually. We all have destinies amidst the interrelatedness of all things, regardless of whether we perceive them to be positive or negative, good or bad. But such trite judgments are determined only within the worldly plane on which we live. Even in the most horrifyingly unimaginable circumstances, all events are part of the divine plan of life. Nothing can be excluded from it. Regardless of manner and matter, all aspects of creation are part of the eternal connection between all things, including the collective divine path of humankind.

⟜ We are but cogs in the wheel of time, souls with visitation rights to play our cards and then depart in the same method by which we came—quickly and without recourse.

If we were able to fully comprehend the roles and reciprocities that exist within this game of life, we might be able to see beyond the perceived inconsistencies and petty lessons of our world. We might see into a world of energy guided by our eternal spirit for the grand purpose of love, peace, and happiness. We already take life far too seriously, but without the subtle joys we entertain, life would be too much to bear, even for those evolved enough to fully appreciate, without rebuttal, each of life's difficult lessons.

᠅ Through our truths, we have the continued opportunity to make the decisions necessary to manifest our physical existence directly on this life-path for purpose, fulfillment, and evolution.

———◦◦ ◦◦———

Moving in Place

❖ ❖

*Time is an equal opportunity employer. Each human being has
exactly the same number of hours and minutes every day.
Rich people can't buy more hours. Scientists can't invent new minutes.
And you can't save time to spend it on another day.*
—Denis Waitely

➤ What if life stood still?

➤ If we stopped moving, would everything around us continue
to move, as if we stood motionless as if in the eye of a universal
tornado?

➤ Is it possible that time doesn't even exist in this present
moment, that we don't move but everything else is in perpetual
motion around us?

➤ What if our perception of reality led us to believe in progression and transformation?

THE GREATEST ANOMALIES OF EXISTENCE ARE TIME AND OUR
own perception of reality. Everything, from the smallest organisms

to the largest minerals, from microscopic molecules to the planets and solar systems, are moving continuously without pause. Although our subtle perceptions do not allow us to see the movement of reality throughout the course of time, everything at every moment is in some sort of transition, en route to some destination.

⤳ Although some people insist that we all move forward; it is the simple fact that we move in any capacity combined with our inability to recreate a previous moment or consciously to create a future one that offers a certain permanence.

We really don't move, and we don't progress; we simply adapt in place as if on proverbial treadmills of time. Segments of time, based entirely on our perceptions, altered by chance or intention, whereby nothing really changes, and time stays the same. Our world undergoes continual evolution, yet is indifferent to it. We cannot stand in one place because we are always moving through an eternally and inevitably positive evolution, in one way or another. It is our mere acceptance of the continual transformation and our attempt to justify and control it that gives meaning to our perception of time itself. Our position in life is predicated initially upon our starting location, and throughout time it is our perceived locality throughout the course of our existence.

⤳ We begin purely as a thought, as a simple gleam in the eyes of a man and a woman; and when we die, we become only a memory.

We travel from point A to B, from point B to C, and all the way to Z and an infinite number of locations across our worldly experience, yet we end in exactly the same place as we began, point A. Total distance traveled is more than we could ever calculate or imagine; yet the total displacement is zero. We come from this earth as spiritual beings part of this physical experience, this physical world, and in the end we depart in like manner. We end in exactly the same place we began—physically it is as if we are created from nothing, and we disintegrate and vanish in like manner. In society, we are really "going" nowhere, for we have nowhere to go. We are actually "doing" nothing, for we have nothing to do. The timeline of our existence is truly outside of our control, yet we move through life with full knowledge of this terminal ailment we affectionately refer to as death.

∾ The painful reality is that every moment takes us one step closer to death.

Although the grander picture of society seems to suggest otherwise, the progression of time does not revolve around failure and pain. We frequently make haphazard decisions regarding our lives, confined by an existence managed around time, pain, and oppression or around love, joy, and excitement, until eventually it all comes to an end.

We must simply release our agendas, our pains, our concerns, and our worries in order to appreciate fully what is available to us in every moment. We must release our agenda in order to truly appreciate the opportunity presented before us in the moment, for only then will we realize that even the manifestations of a lifetime net exactly zero. All we have and all we are is what we share from within each moment.

∾ We take nothing with us but our soul's history and leave nothing behind but memories.

Blink of a Life

He who has a why to live can bear almost any how.
—*Friedrich Nietzsche*

> ⤳ Is life really short? How do we determine if life is actually "too short"?
>
> ⤳ How long must life be for it to be long enough?
>
> ⤳ Do our high expectations prevent us from fully appreciating what we have?
>
> ⤳ What is true independence and does our life actually depend upon those around us?

DO THE GOOD REALLY DIE YOUNG? IF SO, WHAT DOES THAT say about the rest of us? The quality of our being is not a function of the inception or termination of our physical existence, nor the length of our life. The quality of our being is a function of the quality we experience within every moment, our commitment to follow our path, and to listen to our inner truth. The fulfillment of our life is a function of the outside impact we make along the way ... the visible impact and even the reverberations of our actions that occur far beyond our comprehension. Regardless of the choices we make, we need to open our heart to others, to love and to cherish, for ultimately these people eventually leave us either by default or by choice. The emotional body is plagued by insecurity, and as a result, we must continually support ourselves and each other in the *becoming* of our true selves, in allowing our hearts and souls to speak directly to one another.

⤳ We are constantly tested and pressed hard for growth, yet we must create the space for greatness in every moment.

Time as a metric cannot realistically gauge life because life itself exists beyond time. Our ability to follow our path in life is more than what we can achieve in the time allotted, but it is within our ability to stay true to our purpose regardless of the time available to us. Life can never be too long or too short, for a comparative judgment on life itself serves no purpose. Life simply is; it exists for the purpose of every one of us, and we will experience time in whatever manner available, in every moment we are present. We will fill whatever time we have with the choices we make as opportunities present themselves, for that is the path of humankind.

⤳ Within this physical reality, life is truly short, but so are the fuses of human emotion.

As a society, we allow ourselves to be hurt, which forces us to grow and allows us to become the resource for all we are destined to become. This foundation of independence allows us to create relationships not purely from need, but from the potential to obtain growth, happiness, and bliss. We seek abundance in all areas of being, including but not limited to time, money, love, happiness, self-expression, giving, receiving, and even smiling.

We desire abundance in our ability to grow and create, breathe and stretch, dream and live. We desire abundance in our hopes and desires, in our passions, romances, travels, rest, exercise, deep meaningful friendships, success, connectedness, intuition, family, sharing, cooking, laughing, crying, intimacy, wisdom, amazing moments—and in the all-encompassing crossroads of the eternal life continuum. We have much in our lives now to be thankful and grateful for. Our roads are paved, yet it is our choice to walk, run, or even skip along. It is our own personal road, our own proprietary path. The only thing that truly counts is how we show up and what we experience along the way.

⤳ Our time in this place is truly perfect for us and for everyone else, and it is the quality of the moment that determines the greatness of our existence.

Illness

Why do we get sick?

What can we learn from sickness?

Why don't we stop doing the things that make us sick?

Are we ever truly well?

Wounds, Ailments, & History

There is nothing for it:
One must go forward, that is step by step further into decadence.
—Friedrich Nietzsche

> ~ Why is it so difficult to release the past?
>
> ~ Why do we drag the past into the present?
>
> ~ Why are we challenged to release everything that stands in the way of our greatness?

THE WOUNDS WE CARRY THROUGH LIFE ARE SIMPLY REFLEC-tions of our past experience and our history. The sooner we are able to release everything that stands in the way of our greatness, the less of the past we will carry into the moment as a factor of our memory, our energy, and our physical body. Through forgiveness, we eventually have the opportunity to release the negativity of our past.

~ The more quickly we are able to release, the more space we make available for the magnificence of the present moment.

We are extremely powerful beings, perfect by virtue of our imperfection. However, we are intently designed to have restrictive memories in our existence, forcing us to be fully present in the moment. Lingering in the past does nothing other than to take us out of the only moment that truly exists. Just as the storage capacity of our refrigerator or computer hard drive is limited, the experiences available to each of us in every moment are limited by what we can absorb and accept as a function of the reality in which we live.

We cannot change the past, and we may not be able to alter our physical reality with respect to old wounds and painful experiences, but we are able release them while reducing the possibility of carrying our current pain into the future or into the future present. We can release that which stands in the way of everything we are able to achieve, thereby liberating ourselves for our greatness and our future.

~ We are not our past, and we are not our future; we are merely who we are in every present moment.

A memory is never lost; it merely exists outside of our periphery, beyond our physical presence. The Earth itself and every aspect of our universe is only energy. As everything is a function of our reality, and the energy of the universe is ever present, many objects that are generally perceived as inanimate actually carry a memory, a history, and a timeline. Trees, rocks, and even the earth below our feet carry with them a lifetime, a history and energy of the future. Our body carries a memory of its past, and our soul carries with it the lump sum compilation of every experience of our existence. As a result, the natural balance of the universe enlists the participation of all things great and small. At the same time, the universe provides freedom for us to create every experience to our own liking as opportunities are presented to us, but only as a reflection of who we have chosen and choose to be. We truly are one with the world around us, one with the universe.

⤳ We have the power to choose and to be fully present in the magnificence of the moment, while releasing the past and everything that stands in the way of our greatness.

The past has no purpose other than to give meaning to the events that have transpired to bring us to this very moment. The future has no meaning other than to provide us with a purpose for the present moment and, perhaps, something to look forward to in the moment to come.

⤳ The present moment is all that exists—and is the only moment that every will.

Listening to Illness

People who cannot find time for recreation are obliged
sooner or later to find time for illness.
—John Wanamaker 1838–1922, American Merchant

> ~ Why do people die from infection and disease if the body was
> naturally designed to prevent it?
>
> ~ Why do we suffer discomfort and pain, even to the point that
> the pain itself is sometimes more potent and powerful than
> our interest to live?
>
> ~ Why must we sacrifice so much of ourselves to fight the very
> battles put forth before us? Do we deserve the struggle?

THE BODY HAS BEEN NATURALLY DESIGNED WITH AN INHER-
ent immunity to fight off most common occurrences of illness.
The body intrinsically generates organisms to fight infection and disease because it is logically designed to protect itself and fight off that
which intends to harm it. For example, in fighting a disease, the body
will sometimes force a fever as it combats viruses within the body; it

generates white blood cells or increases production of certain antibodies to naturally fight off any posed threats. However, as viruses evolve over time, it seems that our body and immune systems do not evolve and adapt at the same pace. Over time, we develop resistance to the very drugs and antibiotics that fight off the very diseases we resist. How can the body be affected in such a manner as to have its defenses overwhelmed, rendering it vulnerable to disease?

As medicine has continued to evolve over the ages, so has our ability to defend against or render ourselves immune to medicine itself. We create a cure for one disease, and almost instantaneously a new virus emerges within our world that is beyond the realm of available medicine. We cure polio and are suddenly faced with AIDS and cancers we have never seen. Just as we feel that we have evolved beyond the ailments that plague us, we tend to bypass the lessons themselves; and as a result, we are presented with new ailments that either push us back into line or help us open our eyes yet again.

⤙ Through our children we learn that it is often sickness itself that can actually strengthen their immune system over time.

In illness as in life, through adversity we become stronger. As we overcome challenges, we evolve. However, at the same time we also become dependent upon medicine to keep us alive and to protect us as we fight further attacks on our system. From the microbes in the air to the bacteria and viruses carried by those around us, we are eternally on the defensive to protect ourselves. It is one thing to receive guidance to stay on our life-path, but when we continue to suffer as we serve the interests of our soul, our higher selves, and our community, we must question whether our assumptions in regard to appropriate and required service are accurate or whether our previous work is coming to an end. Transitions can be difficult and often stretch the limits of time itself, yet understanding them in the moment can be even more complex.

᷍ Just as every illness has a lesson, every lesson carries with it the potential of illness.

What is the lesson? The universe often creates distraction and impact exactly where necessary in order to affect change in a specific manner. We cannot become overly dependent upon anything outside ourselves for that which needs to be fostered from within. By disregarding the simple hints, the subtleties of truth, and even direct confrontation, often we become sick as our soul attempts to force us to slow down, pay attention, or do what is necessary in our own evolution and destiny.

᷍ It is our ability to adapt efficiently and effectively to obstacles as they are presented that determines the extent to which we evolve or the degree to which we suffer.

Cancer of the Soul

Liberty means responsibility.
That is why most men dread it.
—George Bernard Shaw

> ➤ Why is cancer any different than any other physical ailment?
>
> ➤ We know many of the toxic aspects or habits in our life that we should avoid in order reduce the chance of illness, so why does such knowledge seem to make so little difference?
>
> ➤ With death inevitable for every one of us, why is cancer so worrisome?

AS A SOCIETY, WE ARE UNCOMFORTABLE WITH WHAT WE CAN-not understand, explain, comprehend, or govern. Cancer is malignant growth caused by abnormal cell activity—a tumor caused by irrepressible cells. Cancer, put simply, is a facet of our body that is out of control. We attempt to control the weather, natural disasters, and even life and death. We fear that which cannot be managed or controlled, and cancer exists beyond our full comprehension and understanding.

↿ Physical cancer is nothing compared to its emotional equivalent.

When cancer strikes, it wreaks hell and havoc into our being—but why? Have we ever stopped to think about the spiritual impact or influence cancer has on our lives? We are going to die eventually, so why suddenly the change of pace? When faced with the inevitability of death, why should a physical ailment be any different than the prospect of death from any other means? Some types of cancer can result in death, and others can be medically managed such that we can continue our lives. With physical cancer at least you are alive—with emotional or spiritual cancer, one may not ever have had the opportunity to fully live. Cancer of the soul cannot be treated by medicine or anything outside of our individual self.

↿ Physical cancer is not what is most problematic for us as a society—it is when we are affected by a cancer of the soul, when our life-path and purpose is threatened and we struggle to maintain control over our life.

Cancer of the soul is the result of the complacency we experience in any given moment. It has the power to minimize our contributions, prevent us from making the choices that will better our lives, and stands clearly and directly in the way of our life-path, our purpose, and our success. The only treatment we have is to find the strength and courage to make the choices that bring us closer to that which we are destined to achieve. We must acknowledge and then ignore the voices in our mind that stand in our way, just as we do for people who stand in the way to our greatness. We must stand confident in our resolve when making decisions that move us forward and into health, peace, and a life of passion, purpose, and meaning.

↿ Death truly is inevitable and unavoidable, and yet it is the only certainty we have in our lives.

Our lives are almost entirely uncertain; the only certainty we have is death, although we pretend otherwise. Death is the only aspect of our existence over which we truly have minimal control, if at all. We can choose death, but when death is upon us, we cannot choose the alternative. With this information ever-present, why do we live mediocre lives of quiet desperation? Life is terminal for every one of us. We will die one way or another, today or tomorrow, peacefully, dramatically or traumatically—it really makes no difference. While death is inevitable, life is not. Cancer of the body can be treated, sometimes successfully. Cancer of the soul can only be overcome as a function of our individual commitment. Our bodies can often be managed medically, but our souls can only be engaged emotionally and spiritually.

⮞ Cancer of the body is only part of the equation, for it is the cancer of the soul that takes the true toll on our being.

The risk of developing most cancers can be reduced by lifestyle choices. We all know that we should eat better and take better care of our bodies. We know that smoking is bad for us and that we need to exercise regularly—this should come as no surprise. The problem is that everyone *knows* that smoking harms those who smoke and those around them, yet they smoke anyway. In order to consciously choose to make positive changes with respect to our physical being, we must also face the emotional, intellectual, and spiritual aspects of our being, and most importantly, our core purpose for being. We must truly and honestly love ourselves in order to feel worthy of caring for ourselves.

Some of us are faced with cancer or other ailments, giving us the opportunity to make changes in our lives in this very moment. For the rest of us, we can either wait for some external event to force change in our lives, or we can voluntarily choose greatness in this and every moment to come. Let's not wait for death to confront us directly, but instead let us confront ourselves; let us face every aspect of ourselves. Let us choose not only to evolve physically, but in every other way possible, as well.

〜 Step away from normalcy and become unpredictable; move from complacency to greatness; transcend mediocrity into excellence.

Fear

What are we afraid of?

Is our fear real or imaginary?

Is our fear worth its consequence?

Security & Fear

> ↜ What are we afraid of?
>
> ↜ Why are we afraid to release the past or to release aspects of
> ourselves that no longer serve us?
>
> ↜ Why do we need to feel secure?

FEAR IS NOT NECESSARILY RESTRICTED TO THE PHYSICAL realm, but substantially extends to the emotional and spiritual realms. By its very nature, fear is generally irrational because it relates to something outside our control. We spend money on insurance in an attempt to control or manage outcomes that are almost entirely outside of our control. We purchase insurance for our health, body and mind, not to mention personal dental, life, disability, home, car, pet, and then of course commercial insurance including liability, errors and omissions, and malpractice. What has our world come to when we are afraid to live and spend significant sums of money to protect that which we are afraid to lose? How is it that we live in a society that so covets what we earn? How can we protect every aspect of our being?

~ Our need for security is simply based upon a fear of the future, of the unknown, of what may lie ahead.

We are merely caretakers in this life, with only time at our disposal. At the moment of our birth, we have absolutely nothing, except our soul, our mind, and the body we have been given—in truth, the most valuable assets of our estate. We slowly amass items of a physical nature to which we attribute considerable value and protection. We acquire "things," man items that are designated with a perceived value far beyond their actual worth. We move through life with a constant fear of losing the physical things we have worked so hard to obtain, things that didn't even exist when we began this journey. The irony is that the items of greatest value—our body, mind and soul—are often valued less as demonstrated by how we care for them. In reality, nothing "belongs" to us, for everything is a part of this world.

~ The truth is that we cannot protect or covet something that we don't truly own.

If money weren't the focus of our existence and we were so inclined, we might choose a life of simplicity and voluntary poverty. But money is an inevitable aspect of this physical world. It is a means to an end; although more often it is simply a distraction.

~ We have only what we maintain from within.

Life has become unnecessarily complicated as a result of the value we place on our possessions. As we accumulate, we become protective and fearful, absolutely contrary to whom we are meant to be as spiritual beings experiencing this physical world. We are at risk whenever we possess something that somebody else desires. And the ultimate desire, money, makes life complicated in a multitude of ways, bringing with it the illusion of success and the misapprehension of its ability to fulfill the void within each of us.

⁊ The more attached we become to material possessions, the greater our potential loss, for we will eventually lose everything, negating all that we feel we have "achieved" in this lifetime.

There is no fear beyond this physical existence, for it is limited to this plane to this experience. As a spiritual being, fear does not exist, for in truth, there is nothing to fear.

Fear & Losing It All

Nothing in life is to be feared.
It is only to be understood.
—Marie Curie

> ~ How can we live a fulfilled life while being afraid of losing everything we have and everything we are?
>
> ~ How can we be a conscious part of our greater communities if we are frightened, fearful, or worried?
>
> ~ Can we evolve if we are afraid?

WE LIVE OUR LIVES IN FEAR OF LOSING IT ALL, WHATEVER IT is that we have, and that distracts us from focusing on what really matters. The burdens we carry are surrounded by the most intense and irrational fears; fear of failure in life, in business, or generally in the world around us. Perhaps we are afraid that we won't be liked or loved or that we will lose everything we have worked so hard to obtain or achieve.

~ When we are young we can be fearless because there is nothing to lose except that for which we place minimal value—ourselves.

As we become contributing members of our society, we obtain things such as cars and a home, and we make commitments to a career, to a relationship, and perhaps marriage and children. All of a sudden, we have everything to lose and the risk of failure outweighs the potential reward of moving forward in life. We shudder in our own footsteps, often unable to take the risks required for continued growth and evolution. Such crossroads are our opportunities to step forward into the future, to evolve and become who we know ourselves to be. We must not be afraid of releasing the past or moving into the future.

And beyond all of these fears, there is the fear of not being loved—of losing our money, career, or our home, and looking into the eyes of our spouse or our children to discover whether they will continue to love us for who we really are. Can we still love ourselves?

~ We are afraid to look ourselves in the eye and still love the being within, to see beyond the minutia to our true purpose in life.

None of it really matters; not the fear, the insecurity, or the trite physicality. The simplicity of life itself is focusing not on what we are afraid to lose, but what we have and what we truly desire, our connection to those around us and the fulfillment of our purpose in life. We cannot predict the future, nor can we fully understand the path we follow, but nonetheless, we must relinquish that which stands in the way of our greatness. As difficult as can be, we must focus on what is most important: to love and be loved, to live as fully as possible, to be of service to ourselves and to others, and to let go of everything else.

~ Our fear of loss prevents us from obtaining what we truly desire.

A life of fear is a lackluster existence; it may be a life of incredible potential, but in the end there will be nothing but disappointment and sorrow. We cannot go to bed at night dreaming "what if," and "if only," and "one day." We can only rest peacefully trusting and knowing that we did everything we possibly could in every moment possible; we showed up and gave the world our very best.

~ Life is not a reflection of output or input; it is merely a reflection of the quality we experience and share in every waking moment.

Our children rarely learn from what we choose to teach them; they learn by observing who we are in the world and how we live our lives. Let's not demonstrate pettiness and mediocrity, but instead showcase our greatness, our passion for life, and our commitment to serve.

Energetic Attraction

Every time you don't follow your inner guidance,
you feel a loss of energy, loss of power,
a sense of spiritual deadness.
—Shakti Gawain

➤ Do we really attract what we fear? Does avoiding something actually draw it closer to us?

➤ How do we manifest only the positive energies within our world?

➤ How do we control the energy of intention?

AVOIDANCE GRANTS CREDENCE AND IN SOME WAY ACTUALLY attracts what we attempt to exempt from our lives simply by attaching to it and holding it within our consciousness. Our fears are held in our mind, our consciousness, and our energy field, and are actually drawn into our reality, whether physically or perhaps mentally or emotionally. Our adamant desire to avoid certain aspects of our existence brings our attention and focus to that which we oppose, thus welcoming it into the reality of our existence, even if only within ourselves.

A psychic will read our energy field and may observe the potential for our future as a function of the possibilities existent within our being at any given moment. They may see those energies that we attempt to attract and those that we abhor by our simple focus upon them. By attempting to deny ourselves a certain experience, even if it is perceived as negative, we will inevitably attract it into our experience.

ᐳ We must have clarity within our mind to focus on the positive, on the beauty and magnificence around us, if that is what we desire.

The same energy that magnetizes what we abhor also serves to attract our desires. The power we hold as individuals is more than we can imagine. Wealth begets more wealth; poverty begets more poverty. It is a simple reflection of our ongoing focus and consciousness. It is the energy of intention and action combined that is the foundation of all transformation. It is this focus that maintains our true evolutionary potential, individually and communally. From a societal perspective, the vibration of energy is such that intention and effort toward a specific goal will attract others to the same aspiration and potential outcome. For example, when bidding on a property, coming up with a business idea, or purchasing an item on closeout, we put forth energy into the universe. By putting forth that focused energy toward a specific goal, it creates a motion within the universe that attracts those of like-mind. Alternatively, perhaps, the outcome itself magnetizes those of like-mind to solve the problem and maintain an ongoing balance.

ᐳ The energy of the universe knows no boundaries and has no limit with regard to distance, geography, or time.

We have the opportunity to act upon our insights as they come to us, following our path and purpose in life, to serve our greater communities, and to honor our being and those who guide us along the way. It is within our ability to ignore and disregard that which we abhor, that which we fear, that which detracts us from our truth or stands in the way of our greatness, and to focus instead on the magnificence within and around us. Our ability to manifest what we desire is in direct correlation to our ability to take action with clarity, focus, and intention.

Environment

Who is in control of our environment?

How connected is our internal environment, our INvironment, to our external environment?

Why don't we take responsibility for the environment where we live?

Toxic Living

———◆◆———

꙳ Are we blind to our world?

꙳ How can we expect to be highly tuned, powerfully fulfilled, contributing individuals while feeding the immaculate and extremely complex organism of our being (our body) toxic materials and chemicals?

꙳ We need to fuel airplanes with expensive, refined jet fuel for optimum performance, but why do we fill ourselves with over-processed food sludge?

WE DEMAND SO MUCH FROM OURSELVES AND THOSE AROUND us. We expect output to have no impact on input when, in fact, they are co-dependent in every area of our life. We wouldn't put grime and low-quality gasoline into the gas tank of the space shuttle and expect it to carry us safely around our galaxy. Nonetheless, we put fast food, high fructose corn syrup, toxic chemicals, and hormone-infested animal products into our bodies and somehow still expect to have the stamina and clarity to become leaders within our workplace, our communities, and in our lives. We know that fresh food is better for us than frozen foods and vegetables are better for us than fried foods. We need to nourish and care for our physical body so that it can perform as we require for life, love, and the fulfillment of our purpose in life. Beyond our own needs and desires, we are role models to the world around us.

 ⁓ As complex beings, we need to be conscious of what we ingest because it has a direct impact on our ability to give back to our world.

Toxicity occurs not merely in what we eat or drink; it is appears where and how we live, whom we involve ourselves with, and in how we handle the world presented before us. Just as there are toxic chemicals, there are toxic relationships, lethal belief systems, and noxious people. In finding balance, we must look honestly at every area of our lives in order to cleanup, weed out, and empower the clarity and cleanliness we seek. Seeing our lives for what they truly are requires an honest look at every area of our reality. Only then can we make the appropriate, albeit difficult, decisions for the betterment of our soul and contribute to the evolution of our world. We deserve more and we deserve better, for our life purpose requires us not only to act as caretakers of our environment, but to care of each other and ourselves.

 ⁓ The greatness we seek in the world needs to be mirrored not only by that which we seek within ourselves, but also by the manner and method in which we live our lives.

Our reality needs to be a reflection of what's possible, an indication of the potential within our world, an individual and collective manifestation of our truth.

Holistic Living

———◆◆———

No man is free who is not a master of himself.
—Epictetus

- Why are we obsessed with finding what is wrong with our world?

- Why are we always trying to find problems to fix? Why do we obsess about other people's problems?

- How can our external world be connected to our internal world?

- Is there really a symbiotic relationship between all things, between all elements within this universe?

IN LIFE, INSTEAD OF FOCUSING ON WHAT IS RIGHT IN THIS world, we obsess about what is wrong. We fixate upon the problems of those around us in an effort to distract us from our own challenges and perceived inadequacies. As much as we consume ourselves with the tribulations of others, every challenge of our own carries incredible opportunity for ourselves and for those around us.

⟋ Every problem is a symptom for something deeper.

When we go to the doctor for a high fever, an ache or pain or even an odd feeling or sensation, we describe only the symptom, the reflection of the core ailment. What we see in our world is also simply a reflection of our core belief system. Small internal problems can manifest themselves in our external life in dynamic ways, far beyond our superficial comprehension. The issues and challenges we experience in our work or home life are reflections of our own perceptions, of greater principle issues deep within us.

Gauges on a vehicle reflect the activity or inactivity in specific areas of the vehicle, offering little other inherent value. When children act out, disobey, or rebel, it is not generally the act itself that is the cause of concern, but the belief or mindset behind the action that demands our attention. In that same way, we must look beyond what our physical senses can detect because our world operates in a manner and method outside our superficial comprehension. Beyond the symptomatic representation of our own challenges is the truth of our existence and the clarity we require for our own path and purpose.

⟋ Our entire world is a reflection of our inner beliefs, and every experience and outcome can be traced to the core of our being.

Let's not blame the messenger when we face the challenges of staying true to our path or co-existing within this world, for we must look far beyond what we are presented with. Just as we cannot use a mere band-aid to repair a gaping wound, we cannot just change our environment and expect that change to immediately provide us with all that we desire. The problems we see in others are often those that plague our own lives.

What is the deeper issue, the true cause of our misery? Our happiness is not predicated upon our desires; our happiness is a result of our commitment to follow our path and listen to our truth. As opportunities for growth are presented, we have the ability to walk forward with our eyes open and our head squarely fixed on our shoulders in order to understand and assimilate the inner significance of our outer challenges.

~ Our world as it is presented to us is in direct accordance with our inner truth. Our outer world is a reflection of the world within.

If we are struggling to find our truth, we must continue to follow our life-path in order to *discover* our truth. We must follow the symptoms to find the real answer, our true desire. Everything we require with respect to guidance is available to us if we will only ask and listen, opening ourselves up to receive what we truly desire.

Positive Environment

Whether you think you can or think you can't—
you are right.
—Henry Ford

> ~ How can we affect positive change without altering the environment in which we live?
>
> ~ How can we manifest the positive life that each and every one of us inherently desires and deserves when we settle for unsupportive relationships, live in negative environments, and sustain ourselves with unfulfilling jobs?

OUR LIVES ARE TRULY HOLISTIC IN NATURE, WITH DIRECT and constant correlation between our external and internal lives. In focusing on positive improvement, we often neglect one of the most important foundations of our world: the environment in which we live. We focus on bettering ourselves with intense focus on the outcome of those changes, yet we neglect the reality of our families, communities, neighborhoods, and friends. In order to foster success as a human being, we must create an environment for ourselves that is conducive to the changes we seek. We must foster a space of support, caring, under-standing, and respect not only for the people with whom we interact, but also for the physical environment, including our neighborhood, home, car, bed, and even our fixtures and furnishings.

~ Our world outside is a direct reflection of our world within.

Many times we cannot fix the world within unless we make dramatic change in the world without. We must clean up our life space, creating an environment where we have the space and support for the fulfill-ment we desire. We deserve an environment that is respectful of who we are and choose to be. If we were trying to stop drinking, we wouldn't hang out with alcoholics. In the same manner, if we choose to create a life of happiness and gratitude, service and fulfillment, our goal would be extremely difficult to achieve if we surrounded ourselves with people who were miserable, ungrateful, selfish, and empty inside. Sometimes we believe that by making sacrifices in certain areas of our life, such as our work or the people we associate with, we may find higher levels of fulfillment and evolution in other areas. But in reality, we then suffer the martyrdom of our ego, and to nobody's benefit. We often deserve so much more than we give ourselves credit for, but we certainly deserve a community that is supportive of our purpose in life.

Even as realists, we do need to have a positive attitude, but the truth is that we are limited in what we can offer ourselves and those around us. Our environment is just as important as the attitude we select when we arise in the morning or who we choose to be during the day. We have a habit of spending time with people who don't share our commitment to greatness or to the world at large. We often feel emotionally and physically exhausted after spending extensive time with people who are simply nonbelievers, either in a life of greatness or in the simple com-mitment to a life of passionate service. These people drain our energy, detract from our life force, and stand in the way of our living our truth.

~ By consciously selecting the people with whom we choose to co-create, we have the opportunity to connect, share, give, receive, and create relationships that connect far beyond the typical superficiality of our everyday existence.

Maintaining the positive energy and attitude required for an evolved life can be far more fulfilling when we put ourselves into an environment that respects and nurtures our commitment to greatness. We can co-create our existence with those who share our vision and passion. This is not to say that we need to connect only with those of like-mind, but simply that our center, our place of nurturing, must be one of support and appreciation, gratitude, and respect.

~ We can affect change in every aspect of our existence and every corner of our world, but it begins with ourselves and the environment in which we nurture ourselves.

Power of Breath

❖ ❖

What lies behind us and what lies before us
are tiny matters compared to what lies within us.
—Ralph Waldo Emerson

> ➤ We know that we cannot live without air, so why do we pollute it?
>
> ➤ Why aren't we conscious of our breath or how we deprive our body, mind, and soul of the oxygen we require?
>
> ➤ Why is it that in times of greatest strain, we stop breathing, we pause the very system that gives us life?

WE OFTEN FORGET THE SIGNIFICANCE OF OXYGEN IN OUR lives. Science tells us that the body is made up primarily of oxygen and hydrogen, with water itself being one-third oxygen. Athletes cannot perform while breathing in carbon monoxide or living in smog-rich communities. In the same light, none of us can operate fully while breathing in everyone else's exhaust. Fresh, clean air is an essential aspect of any healthy lifestyle, and quite often only found away from our primary metropolitan areas. Unfortunately much of the air we breathe is impure and thus limits us mentally, emotionally, physically and spiritually.

> ~ When life gets difficult or challenging, the first thing we do is stop breathing.

We don't stop breathing entirely, but we go into damage control. We shut down the very support system that is designed to help us succeed, and in so doing, we sabotage our very ability to move through difficulty toward a place of peace. It feels contrary to our natural instincts, but in times of strife, we have an opportunity to pause and to breathe, not only to clear our mind, but to listen to our truth, to welcome the answers we seek, and to give our bodies the tools required for balance and support. In a full breath, we have the ability to release all ills, to liberate stress and tension, and to find our center so that the decisions we make come from a peace deep within. Air is energy; our breath is energy. We need only visualize positive energy coming in, and the stress, negativity, and duress leaving with every exhale, with our exhaust. It sounds so esoteric, yet we are naturally secreting beings, and as such, we need to replenish our energy and release our physical, emotional, and spiritual waste on a regular basis.

> ~ We must take a moment to fully experience and appreciate our breath, for without time to breathe, we have no time to live.

Not all of us have the opportunity to live within nature's wonderland, outside the hustle and bustle of major metropolitan regions. In fact, not all of us desire such a lifestyle, but we can all understand and appreciate the importance of breathing to fill the fuel tanks of our soul. We must breathe so that we may relax into the opportunity before us and make the decisions that are true to ourselves and to our life purpose.

Painful Humanity

Let your heart guide you. It whispers, so listen carefully.
—Littlefoot's mother, Land before Time

↣ Why can life feel so painful at times?

↣ Why does pain manifest itself into so many aspects of our being—spiritually, emotionally, mentally, and physically?

↣ Why is pain a natural side effect of this existence? What is its purpose?

IS PHYSICAL PAIN EASIER TO HANDLE THAN EMOTIONAL OR spiritual pain? What is the difference? Does one part of our being affect the other? If we are hungry, it will affect our mind. If we are sad, it will affect our ability to eat. However, we cannot remove our hunger pains and feed our body and emotional well being simply through meditation, and we surely cannot feed our soul or our emotional being through our stomach. We must heal the aspects of our life with the specific nutrients, support, and healing they require.

⌐ Sometimes being human is extremely painful, especially when we don't listen to our truth, we ignore our path and purpose, and we disregard our calling in life.

Quite often physical pain can be controlled or minimized through conscious decision-making or supplemented with medicine. But emotional pain is much more complicated because personal and intentional management is often exhaustive. For pharmaceuticals to assist us in the numbing of our sensations, it generally requires a dose so large that our personality commonly disappears in the process. Between conscious management of our lives and the side effects of medicine, we live within an engrossed dynamic, all the while seeking lasting fulfillment in our lives.

Spiritual pain is unique in that it cannot be minimized or managed outside of ourselves, for reducing or eliminating the pain within us requires clarity of purpose and a commitment to *be* our truth in every area of our life. We cannot fix one part of our being with another, but none can be disregarded.

⌐ Pain is a fascinating variable, habitually giving us the opportunity to choose: suffer or make positive changes in our lives.

Pain is a tool used by our body and our soul to affect or force change, even though the process itself can be just as painful to comprehend. Although we are beings of free will and conscious selection, we are guided by the truth of our being. When something is broken in our body, we experience pain as a mechanism of communication and guidance in order that we can repair ourselves and perhaps learn from our potential stupidity. Just as a curb is designed to keep cars on the road and a moving walkway is designed to take people from point A to point B, pain has the ability to keep us on our chosen path.

~ It is when we disregard our truth and the guidance we receive along our life-path that pain can become intolerable, at which point we are again given the opportunity to change.

Suffering is not to be confused with pain, for suffering is entirely within our own control, when many times pain is not. Pain can be destructive, demeaning, and humbling, while at the very same time resurrecting, empowering, and powerful. Pain is one of the greatest teachers we have available to us in this lifetime. In this physical existence, our soul is enveloped within our body, giving us the ability to be fully present within this world. Pain has the ability to instantaneously allow us to be present for the realities of the moment, grounding us to the physical world as we gallantly try to distance ourselves from it. As we follow our path, we must look within ourselves and listen to the guidance and structure we are given along the way.

~ We must listen to our heart and our soul, for we are not always given the guidance we desire, but the guidance we require.

Pain is a natural and intentional facet of humanity and something we must heed. It is a tool to assist us as we grow, adapt, and evolve throughout this existence. We cannot eliminate pain, but we must listen and learn to use it as a tool to assist us in making better decisions in order to stay true to ourselves. We must treat the pain where it resides and at its source, whether physically, emotionally, mentally or spiritually.

~ We must remember that everything we require is available to us in every moment, and all of the guidance we desire is right in front of us.

Caretaking the Universe

◆◉◆ ◆◉◆

We do not inherit the earth from our ancestors,
we borrow it from our children.
—Native American Proverb

✧ Why are we too lazy to care for our environment?

✧ Are we naive to believe that our planet will fix itself?

✧ Why don't we take responsibility for that which cares of us?

OVER THE CENTURIES WE HAVE SEEN THE MASS DESTRUC-tion of rain forests, the elimination of millions of species of plants, animals and insects, and we have watched the toxicity of our world continue to grow at an exponential and alarming rate. We have used technology to increase production of fruits and vegetables, while at the same time decreasing their inherent nutritional value and flavor. We have seen the overharvesting of our food supply, colony collapse in bees, an increase in hurricanes and other natural disasters. Thousands of articles, books, and movies have been penned verifying these facts and more, yet we refuse to take responsibility for our actions on the very planet that provides everything we require.

⟿ How long will it take for us to realize that we are merely stewards of this beautiful world in which we live?

We must remember that in the end, we don't actually *own* anything; we take absolutely nothing with us. We are merely caretakers of these lands; we acquire real estate simply for the opportunity to cherish and care for it to the best of our ability, and in the end we simply pass the torch to the generations that follow. As role models, we fail miserably, for if we cannot care for our planet, how can we expect our children to?

⟿ We cannot wait for someone else to step forward and do the work we shun. We must step forward to care for the world around us; it is our job, our responsibility.

If we remember for a moment that our external environment is simply a reflection of our internal environment, our world begins to make sense, as if we somehow find meaning outside ourselves for the chaos we carry within. The inner conflict, confusion, exhaustion, and perplexity are ever-present within and around us. When we find balance within, we will find balance without, and our world will fall into place as we nurture our collective understanding. Balance cannot happen on its own; it requires our commitment not only to speak the truth, but to ACT it.

⟿ Our own greatness is a reflection of our ability to act in alignment with our truth and to manifest our reality with clarity and focus, intention and action.

We can no longer be dualistic in our commitment to our life or to the planet that provides for us. We need to take responsibility for our choices, for our life, and for the world around us. We are not alone, for together we make up a collective consciousness, and it is up to each of us to do our part for our greater communities and for our world.

Eliminating the Drama

*We are in the black theater of nonexistence.
In an eye blink the curtain is up, the stage ablaze,
for the vast drama of ourselves.*
—Herman Wouk

> ᕽ Why do we thrive on drama? Why are we attracted to the
> drama of others?
>
> ᕽ Why do we find solace in others' misfortune?
>
> ᕽ As a society, can we live without the drama, without exploiting
> the inadequacies or deficiencies of the world around us?
>
> ᕽ How do we remove the drama to obtain the facts, the reality,
> or the truth of our existence?

OUR SOCIETY IS BASED ON DRAMA. WE THRIVE ON THE OVER-
reaching reality. We read the newspaper, watch the news, and
listen to the gossip of those around us as we obsess over the peculiar
elements of another's misfortune or altered reality. We fantasize about
what should have or could have been. Why do we obsess about the

drama of others? We focus and often thrive on those dramas and hardships because doing so somehow puts our lives into a better perspective and lessens the pain of our current reality.

> ﹏ By looking at someone else's problems, we temporarily lose sight of our own, and comparatively the challenges of our life don't seem quite as momentous.

The problem with drama is that it is an extrapolation of our reality, and our perceptional reality is already extrapolated to begin with. We create an illusion with which to compare our lives, thus creating drama and expectation, waiting for the right conditions and the correct response. We commiserate and eventually enter a perspective of negativity, only by comparison to our positive reality, but a place where we are often unable to connect to our spirit or to our source. By focusing on the drama of others, we put ourselves in a state that makes it almost impossible to attract that which we desire.

> ﹏ We must focus on the positive nature of humankind for the experiences we share that foster what we truly seek.

By supporting, living, and surrounding ourselves with purpose, passion and service, we manifest by choice and communicate to spirit that we deserve what we desire. By surrounding ourselves with positive experiences and like-minded, conscious individuals, we create an atmosphere conducive to the types of learning and evolution that we desire. We can be of service to others, helping them to see and find what we have painstakingly discovered. We continually reconnect with those around us and with ourselves, rediscovering our reality, finding clarity of purpose and a reminder of the vision for the future.

The good life can be effortless and straightforward, unexciting and lackluster, or even invigorating, exhausting and inspirational. We have a tendency to crave stories of those who suffer, those who are worse off and those who struggle. We absorb the drama in order to feel better about ourselves, to reconnect with our own gratitude for the life before us, as if there were any truth in comparing our life to another's.

↝ We can find joy and beauty in the sharing of magnificence, for living out of the potential for greatness is much more fulfilling than living out of the fear of failure.

The painful reality of our existence is rarely as traumatic as the surrounding drama, the one factor that we inject and can control. Most times we are unable to control the facts themselves, but only our reaction to them, our perception of them, and how they are extended to those around us. Media and news empires are based almost entirely around the drama itself, for it is the drama that sells and rarely the reality: the sizzle and not the steak.

We remove the drama first by stating the facts, removing the exaggerations, and simply telling the truth. We continue by staying positive, minimizing any negative or harmful complaining about others, and doing our best to be open, inviting, and without judgment. We stay centered and present to our reality and the reflective emotions on which they are based in order to respond correctly to the events of our existence. Imperfection is what makes our world so ideal, for mistakes are inevitable, and we must simply do our best to see the world for what it is and to share the positive elements with those around us.

We are all granted the opportunity to choose, thus predetermining many aspects of our own existence. It is not one grand decision, but the little reactions, the simple reflections and the seemingly insignificant thoughts and mindsets we maintain around life's subtle incongruence's that determine the quality of our existence. As agonizing as it is to accept, when life doesn't work out as we had planned, we have nobody to blame but ourselves.

↝ Our only opportunity is to take full responsibility for our thoughts, feelings, and actions, and in so doing become fully conscious of the choices we make and their consequences.

Life without drama is simplicity and can be effortless. Yet ease is often boring, for it appears to lacks passion, excitement, and emotion. However, in simplicity, we find all that we require in life. We connect with the truth in and around all that exists, and in so doing we have the opportunity to discover our true selves. We can thrive on the positive aspects of our existence, and we can feed off the greatness of our communities in order to give back. In so doing, we can become all that we are destined to be.

Reality

Is this life real?

How do we discern what is real from what is not?

Can we predict the future?

Can we control the future?

Can we change the future?

The Meaning of Life

> ⟿ What motivates us? What is our true driving force?
>
> ⟿ Why did we get out of bed this morning? Why do we get out of bed every morning?
>
> ⟿ Where are we going in such a hurry?
>
> ⟿ Why do we do what we do, choose what we choose, and continue about our lives often without conscious thought, seldom taking full responsibility for our actions, our beliefs, or even our reality?

DO WE WORK SIMPLY BECAUSE WE *HAVE* TO OR BECAUSE WE *choose* to? Do we work merely for the satisfaction of making a positive contribution to this macro-environment we call Earth, and thus become an integral chain in the circle of life, or do we work simply to put food on the table?

We work externally and internally, often striving to fulfill the void within and without. If it is fulfillment we strive for, why do we consciously make choices in contradiction to our purpose and path in life? Why do we brace ourselves for negative aspects in a future that is as of yet undetermined and, in doing so, manifest those very fears?

⁓ There comes a point when our situational reality becomes our norm and our contrarian thoughts become the boundaries for our own existence.

We have commitments in this lifetime, showing up for whatever our world has in store before us, beginning with our soul's path and purpose and manifesting in the form of love from the earliest moments of our birth and re-birth. Eventually, we arrive at a point of change, dictated by our environment and by the very reality we have fostered for our own happiness.

⁓ The search for reason in every action, motion, and reality is at the core of a balanced and fulfilled internal and external life; it fosters an understanding of our place within everything and the place of everything within us.

This understanding is the true meaning of life. Eternal compassion and understanding for all humankind is essential, for at our core we are all alike; every one of us is searching for the same things. Even those of us who struggle with our morals, values, and integrity are only taking a different path to achieve the same result. From the beginning of our time, humanity has exhaustively sought fulfillment, evolution, a life centered in love, and most of all, eternal happiness. Despite this common desire, we continue to move through life obtaining just the opposite. We strive for success, financial prosperity, reputation, material possessions, and the fairy tale life. And in the process, we disregard the most important elements of this existence: the present moment and our inner world.

↪ We cannot consciously strive for success, achievement, happiness, or even love; these are side effects of a life of purpose.

What is it about our reality that leaves so many outside desires and necessities unfulfilled? We continue about our lives, always waiting for the next and better moment, concentrating on a future that has yet to arrive rather than on the present moment, the only one that will ever exist. It is this subtle drive that guides the progression and evolution of humanity as a whole. Our lives are created step-by-step, moment-by-moment within a destiny that we acknowledge if only to foster confidence in the choices yet to come.

↪ Because of our education and the state of our society, we are programmed to work primarily for external sustenance as opposed to internal nourishment.

What is it that we really desire in life? We inevitably choose wrongly, sacrificing time with our loved ones, spirituality, and our personal development for those societal achievements that we hope will bring us the satisfaction, fulfillment, and happiness we desire. We strive for success, money, and physical possessions only to be disappointed when we discover that our desire for fulfillment and happiness is not satisfied by the obtainment of such things.

We often operate in a manner that is in direct opposition to our inner spirit, fostering a powerful love/hate relationship. Why do we have selective acceptance of our world, squinting at the distraction of beauty in order to lose focus on the surrounding dysfunction? Making a difference in our society can be wrought with opposition, true enough. But it's as though we give up before we have begun, using our powerful intellect to develop an endless list of excuses for why we have not lived up to our enormous potential. Instead of following our dreams and life purpose, we envelop ourselves in a reality of our own misery and succeed only in lying to ourselves about the truth and responsibilities of this existence.

Those of us in the midst of transition tiptoe around our existence, searching for guidance outside of ourselves. Like children, we fear rejection and intuit a resounding "no" even before reaching beyond our comfort zone. We find comfort in our habitual subsistence, often at the sacrifice of the deep internal passion and truth we know to be our life-path. We make an impact on our world every day; and albeit often miniscule one, but we make a difference in every moment. Imagine for a moment the impact we *could* make if we were a little more positive, accepting, and supportive, and if we were a little more involved in our community.

⤳ What if we were just a little less selfish and more of service?
   What if we all gave just that little bit more?

The problem is that we lose sight of the truth because we get caught up in the specificity; we miss the message as we try to deconstruct the communication or see through the medium to understand the meaning of what is being said. Answers to life's questions come in the most mischievous ways, sometimes so hidden that they are comprehendible only to our integrated subconscious, whose translations aren't presented at the most convenient times—if at all.

Our society is not only based on the concept of individual freedom, but has also accepted all the auxiliary notions and responsibilities of being a First World nation. We focus upon the basics of need fulfillment while, ideally, doing our part for the evolution of our society—perhaps through technology, economics, politics, or global initiatives. By virtue of being alive, we are part of this global community, and we are here to fulfill our path and purpose with a life of service. We are all similar in that we strive for and feel the same emotions as a distinct reflection of our own reality.

Life in its most simplistic state is a quest for answers, for the meaning behind the answers, and for the connection with our own inherent truth that guides us every step of the way. Our lives and the interrelated paths we share with others are the foundation of the fulfillment and evolution we all seek, both individually and collectively.

᚜ The meaning of life is a life of meaning.

The meaning of life is not some abstract thing that we seek to obtain. It is not any one "thing." The meaning of life is simple: it is an understanding; it is our path, it is our quest.

———————————◆◆ ◆◆———————————

Perceived Reality

——◈◈——

Everyone thinks of changing the world,
but no one thinks of changing himself.
—Leo Nikolayevich Tolstoy

~ Why is our external environment so different from our internal environment?

~ Why is the world around us so different from what we see within?

~ Why is our perception of reality often so different from everyone else's?

~ Where does reality meet perception?

Our world is what we perceive it be. Our perceptions control our world, the life we experience within each and every moment. Our perceptions are based on our belief system, which has been developed throughout our childhood and young adulthood. Our perceptions are a function of our educational systems, our families and friends, and anyone and anything with whom we have interacted throughout our lives. Our perception is the filter through which we see our world; it is the basis for our creation and acceptance of the world around us.

⁓ Our reality is what we perceive it to be.

We are provided with controls to determine which aspects of our reality are true and accurate in any given moment based upon what we perceive. Much like a trip to Las Vegas provides illusions of grandeur and teases our sense of desire, overindulgence, and intemperance, its mirage and surrealism conflicts with even the distorted reality of our own daily life. Within every perceived reality, there is a truth, an inner knowing that we choose to accept or to ignore. We have been provided with a world so vast and extraordinary that it exists beyond our full comprehension. At the same time, we are given the tools to read beyond our perceptions and toward a truth that resonates with our heart and soul.

We receive the key to the city of our soul through our coming of age, when we are ready to see and follow our life's path and purpose. Discard responsibility, and we have the opportunity to blame the world for the misfortunes of our reality. Ignore the truth, and we can simply blame a higher power for our pain and suffering. Abandon life's path and we must navigate a life filled with every temptation the physical world offers, but without meaningful purpose and passion, true happiness, and effervescent fulfillment.

We must accept and become the master of our reality, as the adversities before us become stepping-stones into the future. By expanding and maximizing our conscious decision-making abilities, our world becomes so much more than its ordinary pettiness. If you cater to your worldly perceptions and limiting beliefs, your reality will be limited and distorted.

⁓ Follow your heart and you will see the world within. Follow your soul and you will see the world.

If we are chaotic inside ourselves, our outer lives will be chaotic. If we feel clouded within, our outside world will feel foggy, confusing, or overly complex. If we feel abundance, we may connect with our world. If we feel depressed, we can connect with the depression around us. The lens and filters we use to see and perceive our world are determined entirely by our inner temperature. We can attempt to alter our external environment in order to fix the challenges within; however, it is what lies within us that creates our world. We must focus our efforts on the root of the problem, the source of our pain.

~ Our external world is a direct reflection of our inner climate.

Not only is our external environment a reflection of our internal being, but certain types of people have a greater need for external, physical, self-expression than others. For example, artists may have homes that are more reflective of who they are, perhaps with colors and drama. A philosopher or intellectual may have a simple home, reflecting harmony or perhaps organized chaos. Who we are on the outside is a reflection of who we are and who we choose to be within. We must find our happiness and passion within ourselves so that we can *be* and share our truth everywhere in our world.

~ Long gone are the days when we could ignore our truth while living an illusion. We owe it to ourselves and to those around us to live and breathe our truth in every waking moment.

Perception Is Everything

Everything you can imagine is real.
—*Pablo Picasso*

> ➴ Why do we have more faith in our external world than our inner truth?
>
> ➴ Why is it that we give more credence to our perception of reality than to our inner knowing?
>
> ➴ Why do our illusions overpower our certainty?

SOME SAY THE WORLD IS A DANGEROUS AND TERRIBLE PLACE, that it is heartless, unforgiving, and ruthless. They proclaim that this world will give us nothing, save what we take from it. They may be correct; however, it is only their personal perception that gives them this level of understanding. By changing our perceptions and viewpoints, we quickly see how powerful our thoughts truly are, and how easily we allow ourselves to be controlled by the influences of our environment. Our entire world is an elaborate illusion designed to fool the mind and, at times, even the heart.

ᕁ Nothing is as it appears to be.

The reality of our world, of those around us, and of everything we value is based entirely on our perception of it. And our perceptions are based upon our belief system. It is not our thoughts alone that create our reality, for they are just the tip of the iceberg. It is our belief structure that creates the entire reality in which we live.

ᕁ Reality is what we perceive; truth is what we believe.

Our life and every decision we make is dominated by the illusion of this physical reality, whether with respect to the matter at hand, relationships, education, livelihood, peace, spirituality, safety, or even our interpretation of what it means to be alive. We find all of the meaning we require simply by looking for it. Everything truly is an illusion, for we see what we want to see, perceive what we want to perceive, and believe only what we want to believe.

ᕁ Our internal belief system creates our reality in its entirety.

We attempt to comprehend the divine plan unfolding in and around us, often finding humor in our coincidental experiences. We relish the thought of a world so intertwined that every action is connected to millions of others. Actions as trivial as purchasing toiletries or making a phone call are seen to play a role in our divine outcome. We make vague assumptions concerning the nature of happenstance, blaming the master spiritual power and often belittling our control over the outcome of our lives. Is there a superpower, a "being" outside of us that is really in control of our lives? Are we marionettes, or are we strong enough to make our own choices while also being a part of the universe as a whole.

ᕁ We cannot look outside for the answers; the truth we seek is within us.

The real game of life occurs from inside of us; everything else is simply a reflection of that which we hold closest to our being, the genuine truth of our existence. It is the inner game of relationship, the inner game of love, the inner game of life. Accessing this intricate balance of power is much more complicated than we can imagine, for the superficiality with which we face our lives gives little hint to the truth of our true belief system. Accessing our inner core requires a much deeper understanding of everything we value and all that we believe.

~ Evolution happens over the course of our lives, based on our transcendence of obstacles and learning that allows the world to unfold naturally before our eyes.

At times we receive glimpses. We experience strong emotions that elicit feelings of shock at the manner in which we mismanage our world. Even as our lives are enveloped in continual distractions—such as music, television, cell phones, computers, traffic—that affect our focus and clarity, every action and reaction, situation and experience is a reflection of who we are in this moment. We are continually sucked into the pain and joy of our manifested reality, giving us the easy opportunity to evade our truth at every occasion. We cannot blame a higher power for the choices we make that create the situations in which we find ourselves.

~ Our dreams are attainable if we can only learn to listen to our inner truth and take intentional action.

We need to take responsibility for our successes and our failures without place blame or attributing the success upon others or a higher power. We are responsible for the journey and the resulting destination of our lives. If we are one with our source, then we take responsibility and are gracious for both our successes and failures, but the path is still ours and ours alone. We cannot disregard what we feel within and know to be true. Failure offers us the incredible opportunity to learn and grow, and as evolved individuals we are wise to be grateful for both life's blessings and its challenges.

Blame should not be in our vocabulary; we must take responsibility for our own path and the associated choices we make along the way. Finding clarity is most difficult during times of despair or confusion, for we lose sight of what is most important and often have a tough time finding the clarity we require. Our focus in low times is as important as it is during times of triumph. It is our ability to stay clear and listen to our inner truth, regardless of outside circumstances, that provides us with the vision and plan for moving forward on our life-path.

⁓ Everything is as we have created it to be. Everything is as it should be.

Self-Medication

———◆—◆———

Reality is a crutch for people who can't cope with drugs.
—Lily Tomlin

~ What are we searching for? How do we deal with the challenges we face in this lifetime?

~ What is it about our existence that pushes us to overindulge or to become addicted to mood-altering substances?

~ Do we lack self-control or merely the strength and resolve to move passionately and self-sufficiently through this existence?

FINDING THAT SAME SENSATION BY SEARCHING WITHIN IS much more challenging, complicated, and time consuming. Our world is not simply what we see, hear, feel, taste, or touch; it is a reflection of what occurs within as a result of our worldly experiences. We obsess about our externalities, our hairstyle, the clothes we wear, the horsepower of our car, the color of our pedicure, the cleanliness of our ears, the smell of our breath, and the whiteness of our teeth. We spend our entire lives searching for the answer to the void within ourselves, and in the end we discover that it wasn't the answer so much that we were seeking as the question. We spend so much time running from place to place that we rarely stop to listen to the truth of the moment.

❧ We all search for the external stimulus we think will allow us to feel and experience eternal balance and joy.

As part of this often-daunting journey, there are resources at our disposal that allow us to cope more gracefully, but not always more successfully. There are more medicinal alternatives available to us today than in previous generations, whether legal or illegal, yet throughout all of our physical existence, we have found external stimuli to assist us. We self-medicate ourselves with legal stimulants such as caffeine or nicotine, illegal ones such as speed or cocaine, or pharmaceutical ones such as amphetamines or Prozac. Whether we use heroin or drink alcohol, take oxycodone or barbiturates, smoke marijuana or take mescaline, there are endless tools at our disposal to experience the sensations we desire.

❧ At some point we realize that we can never be fulfilled as long as we look outside ourselves for what we intrinsically desire.

However, there is no tool outside of us that can fill the void within us. We look for external stimuli, even overeating, in an attempt to find solace in this incredibly exhausting and oftentimes overwhelming world in which we live. We seek and rarely find because the temporary solace we perceive quickly fades until soon we require even more of whatever supplement we have chosen in order to feel the same high as before. We can even take time for ourselves consoling ourselves in nature, but there is no replacement for living our lives and participating fully in this existence.

❧ There is nothing we can digest, absorb, inhale, ingest, or inject that can fulfill, supplement, or replace our path in life.

We can only search outside ourselves for so long until we realize that beyond our core physical and emotional needs, everything we desire is found within us. There is a place for pharmaceuticals or other such drugs to fight depression and a range of other ailments, including insomnia, brain problems, body issues, arthritis, or heart disease. Sometimes the external stimuli do provide solace through some of the most challenging aspects of our existence, whether they are physical, emotional, or mental. These aids are often just the respite we require, but only in order to ease the transition within to the true guidance and assistance we require.

~ Temporary alteration is all we can hope for when faced with external stimuli, for permanent evolution requires far more than an injectable or a digestible.

The opportunity we have is to understand and accept the aspects of our existence that we have the power to alter, and those that we cannot. We can change our feelings or our experience in this life consciously or with assistance, but we will not change the core belief that created those feelings merely through a temporary, mood-altering substance. We can utilize external stimuli, but it is courage and resolve that we require to help us complete the transformation we desire.

~ Permanent transformation requires a connection to our soul, a bonding with spirit, an understanding and transformation of our own core belief structure.

As physical as this world often seems, we have a finite corporeal structure, yet we are merely amorphous beings on a path. We are spiritual beings experiencing and caretaking a physical existence. We will evolve mentally, emotionally, and spiritually throughout our lives, with even our body recreating itself over time. Our body is a tool with which to serve and follow our path and purpose in life.

~ We must utilize our own power and strength to go deep within ourselves for truth and understanding.

Cycles of Human Nature

A useless life is an early death.
—*Johann Wolfgang von Goethe*

> ๛ Is there a natural flow to human life?
>
> ๛ Does our world naturally ebb and flow?
>
> ๛ Beyond the personal evolution of each and every one of us, does our world evolve over time?

THE CYCLES OF HUMAN NATURE, SPIRITUALLY AND THROUGH evolution, defy human consciousness. As human beings of this physical world, we often feel constricted by the physical reality in which we live, and as such, we live solely within the boundaries we create for ourselves. We ebb and flow in life, vacillating between a purely physical existence and the incorporation of our soul and spiritual reality. We continue perceiving and living within the confines of our personal reality, often underestimating the power of purpose, of redefinition, and the true power of our path in life.

↫ In life, we have our intuition to provide insight into the past and the current moment, and we have manifestation to actualize that which begins within our mind and blooms into something that occurs within our world.

If we believe that we are strong, abundant, and empowering, that is what we will be. If we believe that we are poor, frail, and insignificant, that is what we will be. The correlation between our thoughts and our reality should come as no surprise, for it has been proven time and again throughout human history. Our thoughts are defined by our belief system, and our belief system and thought process is the basis for every action we take. In line with that understanding, we learn to appreciate the connection between manifestation, the actions we take, and the thoughts we carry on a moment-by-moment basis. The life we desire must be so deeply ingrained within our being and so powerfully tattooed across our brain that we never waiver. We then live with such clarity of mission and focus that nothing stands in our way.

↫ Our lives will mirror the feelings within us. We will live our world as a reflection of the clarity of focus and vision that we maintain within.

When we are confused or unclear, our lives will reflect that. By taking a clear stand for the life we desire, the life we feel that we deserve, not only will we receive everything we require in this lifetime, but we will have the opportunity to give and receive in more ways than we can imagine. Just as the depth of our universe and the surrounding dynamics far exceed our physical experience and associated perceptions, the ways and means in which we give and serve are not governed by the physical restrictions of this world. Giving is done in ways far more reaching and substantial than we can comprehend.

↫ As we move through life, we continually recreate our reality as a factor of our belief system and thought process, and our life continues to regenerate itself.

Even with the limited time we are afforded in this lifetime, our reality is always in direct correlation to our belief system. The fixed nature of our perceived physical reality is often inaccurate and constricting, preventing and restricting direct evolution on this physical plane. As we regenerate our lives from the inside out, our physical reality alters and adapts, even down to our DNA and bone structure, as our body and mind regenerate themselves.

> ⊱ Our life ebbs and flows like the seasons of nature. In that manner, we are given the continual opportunity to evolve and *become.*

The world we see before us is simply an illusion. It is based entirely on our own perception; yet it cannot be fully understood simply by using our core physical senses. By finding clarity within ourselves as part of this personal reality, we have the opportunity to alter not only the physical self we inhabit, but also our mental, emotional and spiritual being. Our external experience can eventually become a direct reflection of the beauty and magnificence we discover within, and only then will our life accurately reflect our path and purpose, eventually becoming a true reflection of our deepest desires.

Physicality

Are we more than our physical bodies?

Isn't it time that we looked beyond our flesh and bones?

Our body is just a vessel with which to follow our path and fulfill our purpose in life.

Physical Limitations

———— ◆◆ ————

He dwells in us, not in the nether world, not in the starry heavens.
The spirit living within us fashions all this.
—Agrippa von Nettesheim

〜 Why do we identify ourselves with our physical body?

〜 Why is it so difficult to accept the impermanence of our physical existence?

〜 Why is it so hard to see beyond our physicality to the truth of our soul?

THE SHELL IN WHICH OUR SOULS ARE HOUSED AND THAT WE use to achieve our personal goals is specifically designed for the physical nature of this existence. Our physical bodies are the corporeal representations of who we are on this plane of existence, and is temporary and fragile, but acts as a determining force of change in our lifelong decisions.

〜 Our body is not designed to last forever—that is the role of our soul.

As we age, our relationships change as do our eating habits, lifestyle, activity levels, and every interrelationship within our personal world. Our sexual drive diminishes (as it was designed to), and those very energies that were previously essential to our livelihood are transferred elsewhere throughout our body and being. We are forced to adjust ourselves to this evolution by adapting, massaging, changing our focus, and transitioning our energy into other areas of our life so as to take advantage of the immense power and strength available to us. Similar to a magnifying glass, the energy we maintain as we get older has the ability to become even stronger and more powerful as we reduce the variance and focus upon that which is essential to our path.

>~ The more we attempt to hold onto our past or to what is destined for transition, the more we live our life in the past and restrict ourselves from the true magnificence of the moment before us.

We are who we choose to be, and we live the life that we create for ourselves. The intimacy in our relationships, the connections we nurture, and the friendships we maintain are reflections of who we choose to be. We are who we have become on the inside, in spirit, character, and being. We take pride in that which money cannot buy; and we appreciate more than ever the true investments of our lifetime—our friends, families, and our relationship with ourselves.

By the time most of us fully realize this truth, it will be too late. We will have missed the opportunity to reconnect or spend additional quality time with our parents, for they may have already passed. We may have overlooked the opportunity to take time off from work to spend with our children when they may actually want to or are available to spend time with us. It might be too late to choose life, to courageously face or overcome our fears, or to transcend our inadequacies for a life of greatness.

~ The one and only certainty of this physical life is our inevitable death.

We must take advantage of the life before us. Our bodies are nothing but vessels for the manifestation of greatness throughout this lifetime. As such, they are designed to be nourished and cared for without recourse and eventually be released back to this world, for we all have an expiration date.

~ We take with us from this life that which we become and nothing more.

———————◆◆◆———————

Accepting Our Physical Body

Is man one of God's blunders?
Or is God one of man's blunders?
—Friedrich Nietzsche

> ~ Why do we have such a difficult time fully accepting others without judgment?
>
> ~ Can we accept the fullness of those we love emotionally, intellectually, spiritually, and physically?
>
> ~ Why are we challenged in fully accepting ourselves?
>
> ~ Are we afraid to grow old?

WHY DO WE VOLUNTARILY PUT OURSELVES THROUGH anguish simply to change our external appearance? Do our own perceptions really matter? Is our own perception accurate or is it simply an illusion?

~ Why do we care what others think?

Consider the diseases and ailments that inflict our society, including cancer, arthritis, physical deformities, and other natural deteriorations. There are sicknesses we are born with, others that develop over time, and some that are simply a side effect of the life choices we make. Outside the medical procedures required to save a life or are desired to compensate for significant deformities or ailments, we choose purely elective treatments, such as reconstructive surgery.

The physical trauma of surgery is only one small part of the process and is extremely minimal when compared to the emotional trauma experienced not only by the patient, but by others during times of change and acceptance. We don't often realize the impact that such surgeries and procedures have on the patients' loved ones, including spouses, children, friends, and parents. Many ailments are more challenging, and the opportunities for spiritual growth are available more for others than for the patients themselves.

~ We must be honest and simply accept ourselves for who we are inside and outside.

Our body is temporary and will inevitably deteriorate and decease, but our soul lives on forever. Our society tends to breed a shallowness that deprives us of the honesty we derive from being ourselves in every moment. Instead, we walk through life judged and questioned about our beliefs, our physical bodies, who we are, and even why we are. Before we even have the opportunity to vocalize our place within this world, others have defined us for themselves, basing their judgments on the way we look, the clothes we wear, our hairstyle, our energy and vibration, and our attitude. They have perceived and categorized us, using the filters of their own belief system to determine our place within their world.

~ Unfortunately, we will never be able to control the actions and beliefs of others, but as long as we are true to ourselves, the opportunities for greatness, compassion, and understanding are available to each and every one of us.

Aging is a magnificent and natural process, one that is judged and analyzed primarily physically and emotionally. There is a special energy in youth and a great pride in a mature life successfully lived. Our lives and experiences are reflected in the world around us, and our memories are ours to keep. The aging process is inevitable and beautiful, much like an oak tree or a fine wine. As we move through our life, our ability to see the true world around us and to share our truth from within our soul becomes astoundingly clear. We are all blessed and gifted in so many ways; we just need to accept the world as it really is and ourselves in the same manner, without judgment and prejudice.

~ We are perfect in every way and must always see ourselves that way regardless of the perception held by those around us.

Injury & Regeneration

One cannot step twice in the same river.
—Heraclitus (ca. 540–ca. 480 B.C.E.)

~ Why do bones grow back stronger after they are injured?

~ How does our body repair and regenerate itself after it is injured?

~ How do we repair emotional or spiritual wounds? Do we get stronger when so wounded?

~ Do we ever learn not to make the same mistake twice?

WHEN A BONE IN THE BODY IS INJURED, IT OFTEN GROWS back bigger, thicker, heavier, or stronger, although not exactly in the same way, shape, or form as it was originally. When a muscle is torn, the body will overcompensate in its repair to ensure that it isn't harmed in the same way again. How does our higher self know that we are stupid enough to make the same mistake over and over again? In life, when we are faced with lessons and challenges, whether the outcome is perceived to be good or bad, right or wrong, we will grow stronger. When we are wounded in life emotionally or spiritually, we can learn from the lessons before us and evolve, eventually becoming stronger.

～ Often the pain and agony we go through is a form of re-birth or regeneration, helping us to become stronger, more focused, and more powerful advocates for our purpose in life.

When our body is injured, with the right nutrients and healing support, it has the opportunity to become stronger. Muscles and tendons may grow back when they are damaged, and bones grow back more resilient when broken or fractured, but never in the same way. When we are hurt emotionally, we grow stronger, not necessarily in our ability to love, but in our ability to avoid that which we feel caused the pain in the first place. When our heart is broken, with the right nurturing and loving, we learn to love and appreciate even more deeply. When our soul is betrayed or defied, we have the opportunity to learn lessons and grow such that we can become all that we were destined to be in this lifetime.

There are no such things as setbacks in this lifetime unless we choose to be so hindered. We must take everything in stride, with an eye on the larger picture of our existence such that the hurdles of the moment only strengthen our resolve in purpose, truth, and destination.

～ Every challenge is an opportunity to grow. Every lesson holds the potential for evolution. Every experience offers the chance to love more deeply, to give more fully, and to become the greatness to which we are destined.

With every setback, we are prepared for even greater success or, perhaps, more substantial failure. As we become stronger, we are able to handle greater aspects of the positive and negative aspects of our lives, for we cannot handle the extremes of one without having the ability to handle the extremes of the other.

We must consciously choose to evolve, to become stronger not weaker. By overcoming the obstacles before us, we grow. We have the opportunity to choose our evolution, to become powerful beings in our own right, and to find fulfillment and empowerment as beings of divine purpose.

Physical Connection

———◆◆———

Be careless in your dress if you must, but keep a tidy soul.
—*Mark Twain*

⌁ Intimacy? Connection? Sex? Not to demean the pleasure of
sexual intercourse, but are we so petty that sex should overpower other aspects of our lives?

⌁ Beyond procreation, why is it so complicated to transform our
excess sexual energies into something positive, such as contributing to the betterment of our world?

PHYSICAL INTIMACY IS A NATURAL ELEMENT OF THE OVERALL
health and well-being of our society, one that should be cared for
and respected. Providing ourselves and another with pleasure is truly an
important aspect of human nature. However, our society is often chau-
vinistic and petty, grounded in the belief that connections between
men and women must be based primarily upon sex and physical intimacy, as if this were the only distinguishing factor of an intimate relationship. Although we do have physical desires where physical intimacy

is required, the fulfillment of that intimacy is many times less than we human beings actually require.

᠊᠊᠊ At some point the desire for physical connection becomes a distraction from the meaning of a life of purpose, service, and passion.

We seek, admire, desire, and hope only for those short and decisive moments that end before we even have a chance to appreciate fully what we have been given. Both members of sexual union are hedonistically—and many times rightfully—looking for an emotion that will fulfill and carry them through to the next phase of existence. We can provide our partners with intimate gratification, but it must be done without guilt and without either party feeling indebted to the other for granting the satisfaction desired. Physical intimacy is a natural and healthy aspect of a successful, intimate relationship, but it must be in context with the higher purpose of the relationship itself. Staying in the higher vibration, there is no such thing as infidelity.

᠊᠊᠊ True fulfillment and lasting happiness cannot be derived from another; it can only come from within.

We can solve these common human problems by transferring our sexual energies into the parts of our beings that require it most. We all have the ability to transform ourselves from shallow physical beings into powerfully evolved bodies of energy that can appreciate the gift and joy of actual emotions and feelings as they relate to physical exchange. Our society does not naturally instill this tendency in us, for so many marketing and advertising campaigns are founded purely upon petty sexual innuendo. But we need to be bigger, better, and stronger. Basic physical desires come from our lower energy body, from a lower vibration; conversely, our higher selves operate on a level that involves the fullness of our emotional and spiritual selves.

Stereotypically, many would say that most women are in control *of* what would be loosely termed sexual codependency, and most men are controlled *by* it. Truthfully, men are frequently weak and petty when it comes to physical intimacy because it is frequently a primordial desire, while women are often able to focus on higher vibrations and more important aspects of our intimate relationships. We need to connect deeply, intellectually, soulfully, and emotionally so that all of our exchanges are deep and lasting. We need to maintain a profound and fulfilling relationship with others and with ourselves so that we feel peace and serenity in all of our actions. We need to appreciate all of the magnificent gifts that we have been given and the opportunities before us while putting our sexual drive and physical desires on the back burner.

ᔨ Physical intimacy in its most evolved nature is merely a reflection of the emotional and spiritual intimacy shared between two parties.

We must use our sexual energy for good, for it was designed to operate in balance and tandem between both parties. Sex is neither sinful nor harmful when done to the satisfaction of both parties; it is simply a natural component of the evolution and satisfaction of our species, and as such, it needs to be honored. Sexual intimacy is only one aspect of a healthy physical relationship. We need to manage our priorities with one another so that we can move beyond physical pettiness and develop deep and meaningful connections. We will then truly have the opportunity to evolve and experience deep fulfillment and true happiness. The journey is not always easy; however, we have encountered one more place to showcase our devotion, morals, and interests in order to evolve, connect, and appreciate ourselves and those around us.

ᔨ We must use the power of sexual energy to obtain that which we truly desire—connection and fulfillment, growth and evolution.

Physical Detachment

Health is a state of complete physical, mental and social well-being, and not merely the absence of disease or infirmity.
—World Health Organization, 1948

➤ Is this life just an illusion? How do we define what is "real"?

➤ Are emotions "real" even though we cannot see or touch them?

➤ Do our bodies really exist, or are they merely vessels for our soul, vehicles for service and greatness?

➤ Are we our body or are we merely in a body?

AS HUMAN BEINGS, WE FIND OURSELVES CONFRONTED WITH the physical niceties we supply each other and ourselves in order to make our worldly transition more comfortable. We have the opportunity and freedom to clothe ourselves, purchase the most appropriate mode of transportation, and find a suitable home for our families and ourselves, furnishing it as we see fit. We live within the confines of the world we have created, and over time we find ourselves attached to those very items. We not only get attached to that which we have supplied ourselves, but also to that which is supplied by the world around us. We live within the illusion of this reality, becoming attached to the physical elements of our life that have little value, forgetting the temporal reality within which we live.

⤳ We accept our physical body, our world, and the reality in which we live only to be shocked when our physical world begins to disintegrate or is taken from us.

What is "real" in this world? We typically classify those things that we can perceive with our core physical senses. If we can taste, smell, hear, touch, or see something, then we say that it is "real." However, there are those things we consider "real" that require special equipment to see as they cannot be seen with the naked eye ... viruses, energy, and barometric pressure, for example, even though some are able to sense the presence of any number of these. Sometimes our senses lie to us as we perceive something that does not exist, smelling cookies when nobody is cooking or seeing something that turns out to be nothing. How do we classify those things that we cannot see or perceive with our physical senses, yet are unable to scientifically disprove? Are our emotions real? We know what anger, hate, love, empathy, and compassion feel like from within, but what do they look like? Can we really love another even though we are unable to see, taste, hear, touch, or smell love?

⤳ At some point we realize that the meaning and power of our life comes only from within ourselves.

In life, there are those of us who lose limbs or who deal with disease, ailments, or accidents. The longer something or someone is a part of our world, not as a function of time but the significance or the quality of moments shared, the more comfortable we become, the closer they grow to our heart and soul, and the harder it is to let go. As we grow attached to our lives, our friends, technology, and happenstance accoutrements, next to the loss of our loved ones, it is the weakening or destruction of our physical body that will be the most difficult to deal with. From a physical perspective, it is no surprise that everything we hold dear will eventually deteriorate and atrophy without our consent or control. The only certainties in life are change and death.

᠈᠆ Our physical body is not an extension of our selves, it is our vessel for greatness in this life; it is simply our representation on this physical plane.

In reality and in truth, we are merely stewards of our land and our bodies. We are merely caretakers with no control over the outcome, only a role in the management and proper maintenance of our world and the avenues with which to appreciate it. With that in mind, we have a responsibility to take care of ourselves, to nurture ourselves to the best of our ability, and in the end, to release our physical body completely because we cannot control the inevitable. As our body is simply a vessel toward a life of service and the fulfillment of our life purpose, it is designed to be relished, respected, nurtured, and eventually released.

᠈᠆ Beyond the trite physicality of this existence, we ultimately relinquish all physicality so that we can transcend this life into the next.

Self-Sacrifice & Abuse

Diseases of the soul
are more dangerous and more numerous
than those of the body.
—Cicero

⁊ Why do we mistreat or abuse ourselves?

⁊ Why is moderation a concept beyond our grasp?

⁊ Do we mistreat ourselves in an attempt to protect or shield ourselves from what we fear or believe we are unworthy of?

W E HAVE THE TENDENCY TO ABUSE OURSELVES, TAKING advantage of the tools available to us, often attempting to find the shortest distance between the place we are and where we want to be. As a culture we smoke, drink, use drugs, avoid exercise, postpone sleep, and simply don't care adequately for ourselves. We overindulge in the trite physical delicacies of our existence, whether it is sex, junk food or any other form of neglect. Do we gain weight in order to shun intimacy or get high or drunk to replace connection? Do we become emotionally negative or abusive or allow ourselves to become repulsive in our appearance to push others away?

⟆ Do we intentionally sicken our bodies in order to find excuses for avoiding our life-path?

There is something to be said for momentary fulfillment; however, we must care for that which we have been given. Do we not value our lives, or do we self-inflict as an excuse for a lack of general happiness and fulfillment? Why would we choose a path of momentary self-gratification at the cost of a life fulfilled in spirit and love? Why would we choose a path of hedonistic martyrdom over one of fulfillment, happiness, and evolution?

Being a fully conscious human being requires significant and ongoing exertion, but giving up requires only temporary resolve and unfortunately desertion, ultimately meaning death or suicide, often occurring with a life purpose left unfulfilled.

⟆ The loss of a life is simply that, but to quit before fulfilling a dream or our life purpose is truly a tragedy.

We don't give ourselves enough credit for the difficulties and complexities involved in being an active member of the human community. The daily and momentary triumphs and tribulations that occur in all aspects of our lives are monstrous and require our concentration and focus on a near moment-by-moment basis. Beyond that, it is exhausting to make so many decisions, overcome an endless lifetime of lessons, and still find time for romance, family, happiness, peace, fulfillment, joy, and evolution.

⟆ Much of our life circumstances and events are beyond our control, and the parts we *can* direct are not much more than teasers that provide us with the illusion of power, keeping us happy and peaceful in a world beyond our comprehension.

We take life so seriously when in reality we act like puppets on a path within this physical reality, repeating the patterns of yesterday, and not taking responsibility for the choices we make. In truth, we have created the reality in which we live, with a right to create and recreate it as we choose. There is joy, happiness, peace, and love to be found through a combination of giving, receiving, sharing, caring, loving, and being—many of which are extremely difficult to accomplish in the midst of a lifetime of self-sacrifice and abuse.

True service is selfless, giving with the fullness of our being, sometimes without the need for reward or remuneration. Self-sacrifice is not to be confused with service, for self-sacrifice is sacrificing ourselves or harming ourselves out of a presented interest in helping others, but in reality it is by personal motive or fear alone. We may not have many choices as to the actual environment surrounding our existence or the world's reaction to us, but we do have the choice about which path we choose and how we choose to experience our world. There is no comparison between a life lived in fear or trepidation at the idea of impending death, versus a life of true service, fulfilled in love, happiness, and peace.

᠅ We must relinquish our agenda, accepting the aspects of our destiny outside our control, and releasing all our attachment and anxiety over expected outcomes so that we can fully experience the greatness of the moment.

Changing Our Physical Bodies

Good for the body is the work of the body,
good for the soul the work of the soul,
and good for either the work of the other.
—Henry David Thoreau

~ Why are we so attached to our physical bodies?

~ Is it possible to modify our bodies without altering our lifestyle?

~ Why is it so difficult to change our bodies?

~ Don't we realize that our physical reality is temporary and that our obsession with it only limits our understanding, appreciation and acceptance of the world around us?

OUR PHYSICAL BODY HAS BECOME A FASCINATION, AN OBSESsion, an epidemic cause célèbre of our earthbound reality. In many cases, it has become a delimiter or the standard by which all are measured. However, as our reality is bound only by our acceptance of the physical world in which we live, we have been given free will to determine the role, form, and reality our physical presence plays within our greater world. We can choose to focus on the superficiality of our physical presence or on the aspects of our being that truly provide value to ourselves and those around us. Making core alterations to our physical body is never as easy as the marketing messages present it to be. Our bodies are not merely a compilation of fascia, muscles, calcium, and blood. Beyond the trite physicality of our body, we are an intricate correlation of the physical reality that we all enjoy.

~ Our physical bodies are simply a representation of that which we believe and that which we are within this physical life.

Beyond the physical, it is our ethereal and dynamic bodies that many of us are either unable to distinguish or refuse to acknowledge that make us who we are. The appearance we take as babies, adolescents, and adults is built directly into our DNA. The forms we take, the methods we use, and everything about our existence is controlled by the spiritual and emotional aspects of our being. Many times we swim upstream as we try to alter our physical bodies in order to fix or influence our emotional and spiritual bodies. It is so difficult for us to understand that just the opposite is true; in order to affect physical change, we must first adapt emotionally, intellectually, and spiritually. But this is an inner obstacle even more so than a physical one. Making physical adjustments first requires an acceptance of who and what we are, an understanding of our own limiting beliefs, and then adjustments from the inside out, not from the outside in.

The lifetime of stress built up in our bodies from the day-to-day burdens we carry requires more than a mere massage to release. The slouching nature of an emotionally depressed human being requires more than a chiropractor, a yoga class, or structural integration to discharge. The deep internal wounds of a mentally challenged human being require more than medication in order to affect permanent change.

~ We are not our bodies; we are spiritual beings living a physical existence. However, to truly affect change on our physical plane, we cannot be apart from this world, we need to a part of it.

We need to alter the image we hold of ourselves in order to release the patterns that our bodies have accepted as rote, the core changes to the way we handle the experiences before us, and our emotional reactions to the rollercoaster events of our lives. It is not our physical body that defines or limits us or even this physical world; it is our perception of our body or world that prevents or enables our greatness. We have the opportunity to mold ourselves into the manner of our own choosing. We can dramatically change our entire being in order to align it with the image we hold within our soul; we can change our physical perception simply by altering our own vision of ourselves. We begin this process by having a clear vision of who we are, not in the minds of others or society, but in our own minds.

~ The mind maintains an indelible control over the reality in which we live and its ability to help us create all that we desire on this plane.

Beyond our physical reality, manifestation at its core requires passion, purpose, and the commitment of our soul. We must have clarity about what we are trying to achieve emotionally, spiritually, and physically, for we will manifest the vision we hold within our mind. We sorely underestimate the power of the human intellect and its ability to manifest our desires, consciously and subconsciously. We have the opportunity to leverage the full power of our being, matching our physical existence to that which we hold true within ourselves.

Death

I am dying.

You are dying ... in fact we are all dying.

Yes, we are. Right now in this very moment, we are dying.

We are sick. It's contagious, and it's terminal.

No doctor or priest can tell us when we will die or even how we will die, but it is only a matter of time until we do.

Welcome to reality! Our time is limited. We might as well get on with it; so why not choose now to live the life of our dreams?

What have we got to lose?

We must make the decision to choose life—not tomorrow, not later, but right now!

Life before Death

It is not the mountain we conquer, but ourselves.
—*Edmund Hillary*

- ~ Why are we afraid of death? Why are we afraid to live?

- ~ Why is death such a travesty even though it is the natural destination of a physical existence for all human life, the inevitable outcome to all our lives, our physical destiny?

- ~ Are we dying right now? Can we do anything about it?

THE LOSS OF ONE'S LIFE OR DEATH IS NEVER INSTANTANEOUS according to the divine path of every human being. We merely perceive it as such, as much our belief in the spontaneity and immediacy of death as the assumption that it takes place at a finite moment. Our physical body may terminate at a precise moment, but the death or deportation of our soul pays tribute to neither time nor place. Traumatic or otherwise, death has a direct correlation to the coincidental destiny of every soul across all of humanity and the destiny of the universe itself. Just as there is a gestation period in birth, there is also one in death, although we are rarely able to acknowledge it.

~ Death happens throughout the course of existence, in direct relation or direct opposition to the life we live.

The further we have integrated into life, the further along our transition to death; although not linear, the two chapters of our soul—life and death—are inextricably commingled. Neither death nor birth occurs at the moment stated on an official certificate. Our physical body is nothing without the soul, much like a car without a driver, or a seed not yet planted or given the environment it needs to thrive. Our soul does not exist within this physical reality without an associative body or vehicle with which to fulfill its purpose. The body is "birthed" while a soul "integrates." The soul slowly enters the body in a staged progression throughout the pregnancy, birth process, and even throughout infancy until it has completed full entry into the body, creating the opportunity for full consciousness.

~ Our body is negligible without our soul, and physical death merely provides the opportunity for one's soul to progress on to its next incarnation.

Sometimes our soul never fully enters our body, for without our conscious selection, only a fraction of our soul is conscious on this physical plane. We must choose the spiritual connection and evolution we seek. It is through our choices and path that we descend fully and consciously into this physical plain and have the opportunity to obtain what we truly desire. Bringing consciousness to our physical being and to our inner truth allows for the full integration of our soul within this physical plane.

Death follows the same progressive nature of transition, with the soul departing throughout the course of a person's existence, whether the result of disease, deterioration, trauma, natural causes, or choice. When we choose not to live, not to consciously demand the greatness of our existence, we transition toward death. When we choose subsistence and the pettiness of our physical existence, we slowly begin to die.

When we choose anything but our truth or our divine path, we are slowly but surely passing away before our very eyes.

~ In every moment, we are either living or dying; there is nothing in between.

As we are in constant motion, we are either moving toward our goals or away from them, yet perpetually toward our final physical destination. Let us not confuse physical death with spiritual death, for many of us will die long before our bodies depart this physical plane. If we do not choose death, then by consequence we must choose life. Death generally occurs over the course of one's existence. By sacrificing the magnificence and the opportunities before us, we relinquish the very aspects of ourselves that we are here to nurture, that we live for; and inevitably, we invite the alternative.

~ We cannot avoid death, but somehow we have discovered how to avoid life.

Let us learn from those around us and from the lessons before us as we seek every opportunity to experience the fullness of the life we are afforded. By our mere acceptance of life itself, we also acknowledge the alternative or the inevitable. By participating in this physical reality, we accept the inevitability of death by whatever manner it may present itself. We can control certain aspects of life; but not so much death. As deeply as death can affect us, far be it for us to understand the deep interconnectedness or exact timing the passing of a loved one may have on the far-reaching coincidences and future reality of our greater world.

~ Upon death, we should not mourn another's life, but their potential, the life not lived. Mourn the dreams never fulfilled, the opportunities forever lost.

Death & New Beginnings

A wise man never loses anything if he has himself.
—*Michel de Montaigne*

> ↳ What is it about death that is so traumatic?
>
> ↳ Don't we all realize that we are all going to eventually die?
>
> ↳ Why doesn't the knowledge or expectation of death make it any easier?
>
> ↳ Are tragic deaths harder to accept?

WE TRADITIONALLY THINK OF DEATH AS THE *BE-ALL AND end-all*, the finite moment when all life shall cease. This is simply not the case. Our soul continues in perpetuity, as does the world around us. We traditionally think of death as a physical death. But in reality, people die for many reasons during any and all aspects of their lives, sometimes long before an actual physical death occurs.

~ The death of our body is nothing compared to the death of our soul, especially the long and painful path we plow when we disregard our truth for the pettiness before us.

Life truly is a journey. Yet during our steady anticipation of the destination before us, we often miss out on the greatest opportunity to be fully present in this existence. We inherently know the right way to go, the right path to follow, but our tendency toward mediocrity and hedonism often supersede and overpower the truth of our soul … and thus we do really live lives of quiet desperation. Death is one of the most daunting aspects in our lives because it is one aspect that we cannot control, although we desperately try. We change those aspects that we are able to; but for others, we learn that we have no choice other than to accept that which we cannot control. How do we fully comprehend death as an aspect of this reality?

The ultimate physical destination is a physical death. Death is release. It is "letting go" in its most natural form. As human beings in this physical world, our pain from death stems from the attachment we place upon life. Physical death holds within it an opportunity, the magic of a new beginning, rebirth, and re-creation. As beings in perpetual motion, aspects of us are growing in every moment while other parts are slowly withering away. We are living or dying in every moment, which is all part of our natural evolution, our personal path to enlightenment.

Death and dying are given the most negative connotations in our society, especially as we grapple with the "loss" of a loved one. In reality it is not "loss," but rather a release, a transition, or even an evolution. On this physical plane, death and loss are difficult lessons to overcome, but as we move deeper into our souls, we discover the beauty of transition, evolution, and re-birth. We learn to fully appreciate life and those we love without having to hold on or stay attached to them—we can let them go.

～ Let us not forget that those we love the most are the hardest to
release.

Losing a loved one is a life-altering experience, reminding us of the
permanence of death and the temporality of our existence. How do we
recover from the loss of a spouse, a parent, a member of our extended
family? How can we ever recover from the loss of a child, as though a
piece of our soul departed with our tragically departed heir? We have
no choice but to accept that which we are presented, yet we have no
ability to control the predestined outcome.

Our only opportunity is to control our own actions and reactions and
to release our loved ones fully so that we may transition in life, and
they may transition peacefully in death. Release allows us to experience fully and be present in the richness of our physical existence. We
are at spirit's beck and call, not only in death, but also throughout the
fullness of the life we choose to experience.

Death is generally deemed one of physical termination, but it is death
within life that is many times more difficult to transcend and the most
tragic. People naturally suffer when they perceive and empathize with
the long-drawn-out death of another, especially with regard to the
sick and elderly—and particularly those suffering permanent loss of
memory, motor skills, or sensory integration. But this transition is an
opportunity to let go, to allow release, as the loss of these abilities is
most often a reflection of their soul slowly transitioning and departing
their body.

～ As we move through life and our evolution, we are continually
forced to let go of those aspects of our lives that are no longer
working as we desire.

It is through this transitioning that we have the opportunity to release
the old and welcome the new. Throughout the course of life, we may
go through thousands of rebirths in order to become the being and

the person we choose to become. We don't have to wait; we have the opportunity to rebirth ourselves in any moment. Death maintains the magnificence of new beginning, but we have the same opportunity within life.

If life is an opportunity to impact and create positive change in society, does death equate to failure if our purpose remains incomplete after our passing? When our contribution is incomplete due to violence, is death the price given to those who fail to achieve? Although at times tragic, the grand picture of existence revolves around the soul itself and its ability to transgress. Death is not a penalty or even a termination, but a new beginning for the next stage of existence. Death is most tragic if we choose to depart before the fulfillment of our dreams, before we complete the service that is our destiny within this lifetime.

⌇ Death is not an ending, but merely the beginning of the next chapter in our soul's evolution.

We must not fear death, for we cannot be afraid of the inevitable and such a waste of the energy we have available to make good within this world.

Fear of Death

*Too many people overvalue what they are not
and undervalue what they are.*
—Malcolm S. Forbes

> ๛ Does living in fear of death actually achieve anything?
>
> ๛ Can we truly experience the present moment if we live in fear
> of the one to come?
>
> ๛ What are we afraid of?

LIVING EACH MOMENT IN FEAR OF DEATH DEFEATS THE VERY purpose of living. We must choose life, but we need not choose death for it awaits us quietly in the shadows. We can die a slow and painful death throughout all our existence or we can live fully in every moment and transition when the time is right. Choosing life is more than getting out of bed each morning to attend to a life of subsistence and subservience. To choose life is to live a life of truth and meaning in every moment, in every decision, to the fullness of our reality. To choose life is to choose greatness, to show up in every way, and to be the magnificence in every area of our lives that we inherently know ourselves to be.

⁊~ Death is inevitable, but living is not.

Our life cannot be determined by the world in which we live, the obstacles we face, the government we elect, or even by our surroundings. Our life can only be lived through our own fullness of being, through the experiences of truth in our own existence. Our world is merely a function of our ability and choice to live our truth in every moment and with every opportunity that presents itself.

⁊~ Our life cannot be lived by doing, but only by being.

We cannot have birth without death; we cannot have right without wrong, and we cannot have life without death. We cannot have anything in life without an acknowledgement of its polar opposite, for everything in our world is in eternal balance and equilibrium at all times.

⁊~ By accepting the inevitable, we have the opportunity to appreciate fully that which stands before us.

In terms of this physical existence, death is simply the next stage in the evolution of our soul. Why are we afraid of death? We are often afraid of what we cannot explain, of the unknown, and what we cannot control. We fear what we do not understand, what we cannot decipher, and those things that exist outside the day-to-day consciousness in which we operate our lives.

⁊~ Fear is limited only to perceptions of reality within this physical existence.

We must have faith and trust in that which exists outside our comfort zone. Those mysterious elements of our existence that are unfamiliar to us are often the reflections of the perfection we seek. When our heart is connected to our soul, our source, to spirit, we are not afraid, for we inherently understand that there is nothing to fear.

Imminent Death

A man dies still if he has done nothing,
as one who has done much.
—Homer

~ Why do we try to avoid the inevitable?

~ With free will and freedom of choice, shouldn't we have the
ability to change any aspect of our existence?

~ Why do we fear that which we cannot control?

~ Are we afraid to die?

WE CAN POSTPONE, DELAY, OR EVEN PAUSE THE REALITY OF
our existence, but our true destination never changes. There are
aspects of our reality that we are able to control and the rest we must
simply accept. We can control our actions and reactions to our world,
to the outer events as they occur around us. Sickness, disease, pain, and
death are merely blips along the lifeline of our existence, arriving at
various intervals throughout our life. But we can only accept or reject
the opportunities as they are presented to us.

~ As much as we try, we cannot avoid the inevitable.

Sometimes we can prevent or postpone sickness, but we are unable to control the lesson behind it or the true opportunity for our own growth. We must adjust to meet the demands of our existence as we continue to be presented with new challenges. We may think that we can postpone death as much as we control a personal exodus, but when it is our time, we have no choice but to go. We all know our destination, for it is equal among us, but it is the path we take that determines the eminence with which we experience our lives. It is who we choose to be along our life-path that sets us apart.

~ Our destinations are equal, but it is the quality of every moment that determines the quality of our existence.

While focusing on the quality of our life, our destiny and life-paths will precede any free will we may be able to exert. Our individual choices make up our reality, but it is the assimilation of all of our choices within this life and our destiny that are the basis for our soul's path within this lifetime. We are given discretion on the manner in which we handle those realities as they are presented to us, but we are not given any diplomacy as to the inevitabilities of our existence or the actual hurdles we may face along the way. Opportunities for growth within this lifetime are inevitable, and as much as we may be able to control the presentation, at their core they are simply opportunities for greatness. Grief, pain, and suffering are sometimes required for growth. If we avoid them in one manner, they will simply present themselves in another. We can try to run from our lives, but we will never get away—for wherever we go, there we are.

~ The experiences around us will rise to meet the challenges of our existence.

Thinking in the extreme, from our moment of birth, we live every moment with the possibility of death. But even with death imminent for every one of us, we still have absolute choice; we have the choice and opportunity to avoid or experience the fullness of every moment. We cannot choose death, for it is unavoidable, so it is our responsibility to choose life because it is a gift that few take full advantage of. As much as death is forthcoming, so are the hardships we will be presented with along the way, including but not limited to sickness and pain, discomfort and mental hardship, anger and frustration. We can attempt to postpone or ignore the inevitable, but we cannot evade it. Throughout our lives, we will be tested and praised, all the while given endless opportunities for growth and evolution along the way.

～ We are judged by the quality of our existence—over which we have been given full control.

A Conscious Exodus

*You will never be happy
if you continue to search for
what happiness consists of.*
—Albert Camus

> ✤ Is suicide really a potential solution to our problems?
>
> ✤ Can we just start over in life; do we get a "do-over"?
>
> ✤ Why is a conscious exodus available to us? Is there a better way
> to survive this life?

WE ARE GIVEN A PHYSICAL LIFE WITH THE INEVITABILITY OF death, but we have only the prospect, the possibility, of truly living. We either choose to live or by default select the alternative. Some attempt to force an element of immediacy: "Today is the day, now is the time!" However, there are times when we cannot even view the options, when we struggle to even face our life. There are times when we may contemplate a different path, a quicker path, one of release, letting go in its extreme incarnation, ending our physical existence in a single moment. Life is conjoined with death; they cannot be separated, for one is fully dependent upon the other.

⮟ Our lives are terminal; death is truly inevitable.

Suicide by its very nature is premeditated. People who choose to terminate their physical existence died long before the actual act—perhaps spiritually, mentally, or emotionally—so their physical death is merely a formality. Suicide is typically defined as the act of physically and intentionally terminating one's life. Physical suicide is symptomatic of a lack of purpose, a lack of meaning, a type of spiritual bankruptcy. While physical suicide is so tragic as to be illegal in some societies, the most devastating and rampant is spiritual suicide; once we sacrifice our beliefs, our morals, and our values … there really is nothing left to live for.

⮟ The true moment of our death is the moment we allow our
    soul to opt out of this existence.

Whether consciously or not, we slowly and physically destroy ourselves as a result of the decisions we make. We are regularly overcommitted, frequently exhausted, and often over indulge in alcohol, drugs, or perhaps an unbalanced work ethic. We grow or disintegrate within each and every moment, for we are perpetually in motion. The emotional or spiritual pain we experience is often the outward manifestation of a life without passion, a life without meaning. But a life without vision is a life without a dream. We die in this moment, in every moment that we are not living the fullness of ourselves, our truth, and our greatness. The loss is not only of the moment that can never be re-lived, but is also the death of a part of us.

⮟ A life without meaning is no life at all.

When faced with a situation in which we are unable to circumvent the physical or emotional pain before us, suicide may be seriously contemplated, appearing as our only option. However, as much as we may feel that our life is over, we may need assistance to step outside of ourselves long enough to realize that true happiness is available to all of us. We need not give up or lose hope, for through a life of passion, purpose, and service, we are able to achieve true happiness—happiness so deep that it penetrates all aspects of our being and overcomes any outside influence.

⁓ We have not arrived until we have discovered our soul's truth within every moment of our being.

If we attempt suicide and we live to tell about it, did we fail or did we succeed? Did we fail at suicide, but succeed with life? Did we win or lose? There are great lessons to be gleaned from traveling through such darkness and desolation. The desperation may last for quite some time until we find the peace within ourselves that allows us to move forward in a world that often seems to err more toward scarcity, power, possessions, and oppression than love, peace, and truth.

⁓ The only path to happiness is a life of purpose and meaning.

Spiritual Bankruptcy

We have two kinds of morality side by side:
one which we preach but do not practice
and another which we practice but seldom preach.
—Bertrand Russell

➤ Do we need spirituality more when life is difficult?

➤ How can children reach their truest most realized selves when they are surrounded by the surreal existence of a manufactured reality?

➤ When do we teach our children to love fully, to follow their path, and to be true to themselves?

ASIDE FROM OUR ONGOING ECONOMIC, FINANCIAL, AND MILI-tary crises, for the most part as a society, we are spiritually bankrupt. It is in times like these that we need faith; we need to believe. When life is great and everything is easy, we often enjoy the fruits of our labors and become complacent. Yet when life presents us with the opportunity to grow, to be and become more, we cannot run from the challenge. We must believe not only in the inherent goodness of humankind and of society itself, but we must believe in ourselves, in our own ability for greatness, to be ourselves and to be of service.

> ᔓ We are not guaranteed nor entitled to greatness; we must earn it by making the difficult choice to become great.

In times like these, we cannot simply point fingers at others and expect someone else to fix the problems and challenges we face, especially when we made the choices that created our circumstances in the first place. We need to look beyond our finances to a holistic view of living that will balance our relationships, our work, our friends, our family, and ourselves.

Sometimes life seems nothing more than a remnant without memory or consciousness, but it is only our perception of the moment that provides us with such an altered view of reality. Regardless of age, sex, race, or stature, the choice of life or death is available to all of us in every moment. There is the potential for strength and passion in every moment, in every stage of life, no matter how young or old our physical body may be. We each must find our own path and passion for life. As our world continues to evolve, we must rely on ourselves and each other for the answers to the questions never before pondered and the insights into realities never before experienced.

> ᔓ We each maintain a unique and irreplaceable role within this world.

We grow up surrounded by a shared superficiality with respect to our greater communities and society at large, and we find ourselves molded to be accepted or rejected by these shallow externalities. Life is often gauged by external gratification rather than by internal sovereignty. We must see through the shell to the greatness and magnificence within each of us and our world. We must know our limits and understand our own constraints in order to thrive and find balance as a part of the universal whole.

∼ We must abide by the limitations of this physical existence, but spiritually we are limitless in our abilities to be and become everything we desire.

Finance

What is money?

Why do we allow ourselves to be controlled by it?

How much money is enough?

How do we meet our needs without allowing ourselves to be consumed by them?

How do we truly free ourselves?

Money, Love, & Happiness

We live in the best of all possible worlds.
—*Gottfried Wilhelm Leibniz (1646–1716)*

> ⤳ Why is it so difficult to simplify our lives?
>
> ⤳ When did we decide that money was so much more important than happiness or that a big house somehow replaced the need for love, friendship, and companionship?

IMAGINE THE CHALLENGE OF CREATING A BARTERING TOOL SO powerful that everyone would desperately want it, even to the point that some would disregard their own morals and values and even break legal and spiritual laws in an effort to obtain it. A tool that would have the power to encourage obsession and ruin relationships, destroy friendships, segment society, create prejudice, and isolate people from each other. Imagine an instrument so influential that it could separate those who have it from those who don't, creating a hierarchical barrier between those who are considered fortunate in society and everyone else.

⤳ That tool exists today and is as powerful as ever: money.

Money is an anomaly, a seemingly essential part of our society's health and structure, yet it also nurtures the more contemptible, deceptive, and corrupt. Money provides access to power, providing the ego with its greatest instrument for transformation. Stigma aside, utilizing money as a resource has the potential to provide some of the greatest good in our world.

~ Money has the potential to destroy lives, incite war, and distract us from what is most important in life.

Money itself is not bad; it is what we do with it and how we obtain it that can be problematic. We can spend our entire lives working to accumulate it, and no amount will ever be "enough." How much money determines the appropriate level of success or achievement? Why do we obsess about money, even beyond fulfilling our core needs in life? At the end of the day, there is so much to be grateful for.

~ At the end of life, health, love, and happiness are the most valuable assets of our estate.

There is no estate tax that can take away the love we carry for those closest to our heart. Many families are torn apart by the grasping for belongings left behind by our dearly departed. We use possessions in a vain attempt to hold onto the past as we deal the feelings of loss in the wake of a death. Realistically, though, no material item will ever replace the feelings of loss that follow the death of a loved one.

~ There is nothing physical that can ever provide the internal fulfillment we require as human beings.

Money is at the core of too many divorces, arguments, and is the primary focus of far too many serious decisions. Money is like an addiction, seducing us to leave our families and to separate from our friends as we generate wealth and more wealth, often at the expense of others and ourselves. Ironically, money also has the ability to help people, to feed the hungry and assist those in need. Unfortunately, we use it predominantly in the wrong ways, living lifestyles far beyond our means that perpetuate the eternal need for additional riches.

⌁ There is never enough money for all that we desire, but there are ample funds for all that we require.

Having more money somehow requires a larger home, a newer vehicle, and a more exclusive and romantic vacation. More money requires a more abundant lifestyle and more powerful friends, or so our society teaches us. Happiness and fulfillment is not something we can obtain or achieve, but is a side effect of a life of service, a result of a life committed to greatness.

⌁ We cannot sacrifice our life and soul in one area of our existence in an attempt to redeem ourselves in another.

The lifestyle of our choosing is a derivative of the passion within our existence that provides the prosperity we desire. More money could require fewer possessions, and greater abundance could allow for greater simplicity. Greater simplicity could provide the opportunity for true happiness, which seems so elusive. Money does not deliver happiness. The path to greater financial acquisition is generally not a happy one; it is everything but money that provides the surer pathway to enlightenment and fulfillment.

Money is clearly a necessity in our society, but it need not control us nor stand in the way of the greatness we inherently desire and deserve. Money cannot go with us when we die, nor can it provide any sort of sanctity or resolution upon our death.

⌁ Money is a tool for satisfying our core needs, for obtaining the physical possessions and services we desire. But fulfillment is a side effect of a service-filled life.

Financial Wellness & Happiness

If you have health, you probably will be happy,
and if you have health and happiness,
you have all the wealth you need, even if it is not all you want.
—Elbert Hubbard

- Why does money have so much power over us?
- What is it about money that leads us to believe it will bring us happiness? Can it actually provide us with happiness?
- Can we postpone our happiness for a future date while we accumulate the money we require?

IF THERE WERE ONE CORE AND ONGOING DESTRUCTIVE DESIRE common to all of humanity, it would be our relentless desire for money. Money is one of the ultimate tests of relationships, partnerships, friendships, camaraderie, connectedness of any kind, and a key spiritual opportunity for growth within our lifetime. Our planet appears to be managed by the financial transgressions of society, although there are grander and more fulfilling motives to support the evolution of our collective consciousness. The pettiness of financial burden parlays mistrust into the inner workings of our world.

Money was designed as a tool to assist trade and to advance our community beyond the barter system, providing an alternative method for fulfilling our material requirements and desires. Money provided the unique benefit of removing the direct exchange of goods and services and, instead, provided a monetary symbol that could be exchanged for goods and services at a later date.

⮑ Money gives us the ability to postpone gratification, but it cannot provide gratification itself.

In modern society, money has become more than just a tool to aid and support daily interactions; sadly, it has become the ultimate delimiter between those who have and those who do not, between success and failure, and is a determiner of health, happiness, rebellion, and violence.

Can money truly determine our level of happiness? Absolutely not. But our society seems to believe it can. Many of our wealthy suffer from a lack of fulfillment or are simply unhappy, while many communities in Third World countries have found fulfillment and happiness by focusing on what really matters in life. Money on its own cannot buy happiness, nor does happiness beget money, although it can often attract it. For humans, money can provide the ultimate separation from happiness and fulfillment.

Money is limitless because we can always obtain more in an infinite number of ways, whether by work or trade, giving or receiving, or through the sale of goods and services. We can save and store money for a later date in a futile effort to postpone or extend satisfaction and fulfillment. Unfortunately, we are unable to stockpile, allocate, or distribute happiness, and our only opportunity is to experience fully that which is available to us in the moment.

Because our world revolves in large part around financial subsistence, it has become the basis for one of our key lessons about growth and evolution. We must all learn that money is merely a tool for the successful support of our goals and desires as physical beings living within a greater society. We evolve on numerous occasions and in many ways, but until we conquer and overcome our own identity as it relates to financial wellness, at some point we inevitably return to our currently available funds and allow them to determine our level of fulfillment and success. Oftentimes, it is our perceived lack of funds that take us to a place of scarcity, providing us with the opportunity to evolve yet again.

~ Until we master our relationship with money, we are held captive by its energy, with freedom eternally beyond our reach.

True eternal freedom extends beyond money, beyond desire itself; it exists where self-determination intersects with our path and where the choices we make are in full alignment with our truth.

The Energy of Money

Be moderate in order to taste the joys of life in abundance.
—Epicurus

~ Why does the attainment of money fail to provide us with a sense of fulfillment?

~ What is it about the energy of money that allows it to control much of our external world?

MONEY IS THE BLOODLINE OF THE WORLD AS WE KNOW IT, providing a means of operation for society. Having an energy and path only unto itself, money influences those who carry or desire it in ways incomprehensible to the rest of humankind. Quickly becoming a ruthless addiction, some people can never have enough wealth and become enveloped in a lifetime of endless actions and dealings, all in the false hope of obtaining an unquenchable "more." However, we cannot postpone fulfillment for a later date. Money has very little purchasing power in terms of the fulfillment and evolutionary goals of the individual human being.

⁓ Wealth has little or no correlation with happiness, which is the
core effect of purposeful service and a conscious life.

At times, it is those without who go within to exude the greatest strength
of passion, purpose, personality, and willpower. It is quite often those
who seek and obtain the most "wealth" who struggle ever more so with
true balance, purposeful service, and spiritual understanding. Let us
not forget that in time, all of our bills will disappear, and all of our worries will absolve themselves. Regardless of whether financial freedom
comes or not, we must not miss out on the experiences of the present,
for they are why we are here.

The cost of living varies tremendously, depending upon where we live or
whom we ask. What an impoverished soul considers wealth is scarcity
or even poverty to the affluent. There exists such a disparity in perception because we base our concept of livelihood upon our beliefs about
life through society. Beyond fulfilling our basic needs in life, financial
balance merely requires a reorganization of our mind and core belief
system.

⁓ We can alter our concept of what is required for happiness and
fulfillment, or we can alter our beliefs about the reception of
wealth—either way our financial reality will change.

Seeking money for money's sake alone leaves us empty, lonely, and weak.
An endless amount of money exists as it is freely reproducible. As an
intermediary, money has the potential to provide access to "things" and
"activities" that can assist us along our life-path. However, an abundance
of money does not translate into an abundance of happiness or fulfillment; they are polar opposites with no direct correlation on the other.

⁓ Money has the power to ruin us because of its strength to poi-
son and infect even the purest among us.

Money is a key to our subsistence, for it can give us access to the realization of our core needs and is a required element for participation and engagement in the world. So we must choose to work with the energy of money without letting it overcome or take advantage of us. Money is an energy flow much like the energy of the winds, oceans, rivers, and other energetic exchanges in our world. We must align ourselves with it, understand and monitor its wavelength, and step in front of the tremendous flow circulating within and around our greater communities. It has the power to rule, control, and govern and, as such, must be managed and controlled.

Money is available to every one of us; we merely need to choose, to ask, and to commit. The energy of money flows at an exponential rate in amounts incomprehensive to our simple minds. Our task is simply to find a pace with it and allow ourselves to bathe in its offspring and runoff, all the while being of service and helping those in need. It is then that we will receive everything we require in life.

⤙ We need balance in all things, and so we must safely manage and control the power and influence that money has over our lives. In that way, we can preserve our intrinsic freedom and stay true to our path and purpose in life.

Monetary Laws of Success

We have no more right to consume happiness without producing it than to consume wealth without producing it.
—George Bernard Shaw

- ~ Why do we work for money?

- ~ Is our financial gain ever worth the sacrifice?

- ~ Why do we make financial investments merely for the financial return on investment?

A S A SOCIETY, WE WORK SO HARD AND HAVE SO MUCH IN THE way of physical possessions, yet very little in terms of fulfillment, satisfaction, and happiness, not to mention love, spirituality, and connection. We work for prosperity while we plan, pray, and hope for happiness. The money we encounter does enable us to make decisions for the betterment of our families, our communities, and ourselves, but it is not money that we truly desire—it is what we feel money will help us obtain or achieve. Money on its own is empty abundance. In a world where the lifeline of society is money, we must embrace its energy in order to actively participate in society, to provide and share in the greater good with all humankind.

↬ Money is neither good nor bad. It is simply an instrument, a tool for our financial success or failure.

As a society, it is remarkable how many hours we work, exhausting ourselves to earn money for current, past, or future expenditures. Equally remarkable is how quickly we exhaust all we have saved or earned with little foresight on impulse purchases. We take conservative jobs for petty subsistence, or we take risky positions with the prospect of a financial windfall. We risk our money in some investments and look toward incremental gains in others, many times disregarding what really matters in life.

↬ We seek balance in many areas, but often struggle most in our attempt to create financial balance.

As we seek financial balance, we look for sound investments that will reap rewards, while protecting our financial well-being. With capitalism as the foundation of our nation's growth and development, we often make investments out of greed, disregarding the true inherent value of the service we provide with respect to our path and purpose in life. Although we have fostered a capitalist society that encourages and rewards new innovation, it also has the potential to corrupt when the desire for the power of money is greater than the desire to serve.

↬ In life, everything we do is a type of investment, its value relative to what is given and what is received.

We quickly forget that money is merely energy with a current all its own. Investments compensate in some capacity, whether financially, emotionally, or spiritually. In the same light, we make emotional and spiritual investments that also provide a return. We are part of a collective whole and as such, our investments should serve our personal interests in financial abundance and monetary freedom while simultaneously contributing to the collective, to the greater good of humankind.

As with all personal goals, investments should serve a dual agenda rather than merely expanding our personal empire. We must take care of our own needs and personal objectives, but we must also grant the same level of commitment to our communities at large, for we will achieve far more for those in need through our commitment to serve. The manner in which our service affects change extends far beyond what our feeble minds can comprehend. Beyond financial freedom, we have a responsibility to commit to the greater good of ourselves and our society, to use the tools before us to achieve what we believe is possible.

↪ We must not lose sight of what is most important.

Exerting for Prosperity

They deem me mad because I will not sell my days for gold;
and I deem them mad because they think my days have a price.
—*Kahlil Gibran*

> ➤ Why do we often feel trapped in our lives, unable to escape?
>
> ➤ Why do we feel bound by the reality we have created for ourselves?
>
> ➤ Why do we seek prosperity?

WE CANNOT WORK FOR PROSPERITY ALONE, ESPECIALLY once our core needs have been met. Shoot for the moon, come back with stars, and our journey will have been a success. Working for money alone results in a shallow existence in which our true life's purpose cannot be achieved. In addition to those needs and desires that make us active participants in our greater communities, we receive the gratitude that accompanies a life of service, which is the highest form of being on this physical plane. Seek to serve, and prosperity is returned in countless ways.

❧ Often we are unable to let go of where we are in order to step forward on the path to greatness.

In order to progress in life, we must let go of where we are, releasing what is most comfortable. Much like climbing Mount Everest, we are forced to leave the safety of one base camp to attempt the perilous transition to the next, or we will never reach our destination. Money offers a comfort level that feels more like a ball and chain than freedom, often locking us into a pattern, a habit that prevents us from taking risks and moving forward. The larger our bank account, the larger our home, the longer our driveway, the more we have distanced ourselves from the world around us.

Progress and evolution require that we let go of where we are in order to get where we want to be, taking risks for the chance of something better. Many times letting go requires giving up a steady income, releasing what we thought our life was meant to look like. Sometimes we need to step beyond mediocrity in any area of our life that stands in the way of our greatness, which may include aspects of our family, community, and most importantly, our manufactured reality.

❧ We cannot make decisions for the sake of money alone because we will never be satisfied or fulfilled with the outcome.

Sooner or later, most of us realize that money has little inherent good in and of itself. We can all appreciate its ability to help us obtain those goods and services we desire, but as a *good* in and of itself, money has minimal value. If we attempt to obtain happiness, fulfillment, or even intimacy or evolution through the acquisition of money and the material goods and services it can provide, we will be left unfulfilled, unevolved, and unhappy. It is when we seek that which our heart intends that we have the opportunity to discover happiness. It is then that we are able to appreciate the true prosperity that is created in every area of our life.

⌁ Outside of our standard need for subsistence, prosperity is only a side effect of a life of service rather than the primary objective.

———————◆ ◆———————

Financial Freedom

———◆——◆———

Freedom is the will to be responsible to ourselves.
—Nietzsche

> ➤ Why do we set ourselves up for failure?
>
> ➤ Why do we spend all of our money and then borrow to pay for things we don't need?
>
> ➤ Why is it so difficult to free ourselves from the burden of debt?

OST OF US LIVE FULLY ENCOMPASSED AND ENCUMBERED BY debt. Our society is currently structured such that we borrow to make ends meet. We regularly spend more than we have, borrowing against our home (if we have a home), maxing out our credit cards, and even scrounging from friends and family to live the life we desire. In essence, we steal from ourselves, from our own future. We then spend all of our time paying off interest on the debt that we accumulated, living the illusion that we are slowly chipping away at the ominous value of liabilities. We cannot live peaceful, balanced and fulfilled lives while carrying such financial burden. Money is not the most important aspect of our existence—although we have the tendency to give it the lion's share of our attention.

~ Happiness, fulfillment, and connection are the true prosperity of the soul.

Why do we always raise the bar with regard to our financial well-being and prosperity? When will we ever have enough? As with everything else in life, it's all relative. How can one family barely survive with X amount of money while another thrives on much less? It is almost incomprehensible that some cultures can survive and even prosper on what others would consider extremely paltry sums. At some point, we realize that there is always a larger more luxurious home for us, just as there are always additional amenities to covet as we move through life. There are always newer or bigger boats, faster cars, more beautiful locales for our second or third vacation home, superior schools, fancier watches, and there are always more places for us to spend our discretionary income.

The problem is that the more desire we identify, the clearer it becomes that something we deem important is lacking in our life—a sensation of poverty exists in which we can never have enough of what we desire. There is only one true way to stop this pattern of eternal desire, and that is gratitude. Pure and simple, gratitude is the only way to change our internal programming. Appreciation of the moment and for what we have today is our only true opportunity for peace and happiness.

~ We can never find solace in our external desires, only in what we maintain within ourselves.

We live the illusion that we can borrow against the future, as if we can repay a debt, not from a financial perspective, but from a purely emotional and spiritual one. As happiness cannot be purchased or obtained, we are forced to find it through connection, love, and fulfillment. We tend to associate happiness with our acquisitions, whether they are experiences or possessions. We must find a way to balance our finances, to spend only what we possess, and to free ourselves from the burden of debt-financed happiness.

The rational solution to free ourselves from debt and to balance our budget is simply to increase our income, decrease our expenditures, or manage some combination of the two. The goal is not only to free ourselves from the debt surrounding us, but also to free ourselves from the stress associated with living paycheck to paycheck and paying out our earnings for someone else's gain. As we seek balance in every area of our life, we must make peace with that most incredible financial force, the currency and lifeblood of the society in which we live.

⨪ Most importantly, we must free ourselves from the perceived financial restrictions that stand in the way of our greatness.

Our society has a much distorted view of what freedom really is as it relates to all areas of our life. True financial freedom means that we are not dependent on others for our financial well-being, for financial freedom is a side benefit of a fully evolved and committed lifestyle. True financial freedom means that we have the opportunity not only to pursue our goals, but also to follow our dreams. We must not see success as something that is inextricably tied to money. Financial freedom is nothing more than a reality we choose to experience, an illusion of choice, in order to wake up every morning feeling that we are everything we deserve to be, and who we are is more important that what we have.

We have more to provide than what is inside our wallet. True financial freedom is freedom from within. This, in turn, alters our belief structure to the point that our reality becomes one of service, and success in life comes from connection, love, and true happiness. It is only then that money becomes yet another tool to assist us in the fulfillment of our lifelong endeavors.

〜 We can never truly be free until we balance our priorities and master our emotions around financial prosperity.

Accumulation

What are we holding on to?

Is any of it really going to fulfill us or bring us happiness?

How can we let go and move forward?

Life's Accumulations

Most human beings have an almost infinite capacity
for taking things for granted.
—*Aldous Huxley*

> ⁓ At the end of the day, does anything really matter?
>
> ⁓ Why do we become so attached to the physicality of this existence?
>
> ⁓ What is it about the "things" that we accumulate that make us unable to let them go?

WE BEGIN LIFE WITH NOTHING BUT OUR SOUL AND THE BODY we are given. For most of us, we were born into this world with an incredible mind, an efficient and highly functioning physical body, and most importantly, our connection to the infinite wisdom of our soul. All of these incredible gifts we received absolutely free simply by being born. Yet our ability to utilize them to their fullest has always been limited by our commitment to take responsibility for our thoughts and actions and to consciously evolve through the choices and opportunities presented to us. Yes, we have received these tools free of charge, yet opportunity is matched or exceeded only by responsibility.

⁓ The best things in life really are free, and those things that cost the most often provide the least amount of value.

It requires a lifetime to realize that the more expensive the toy, the less true value or positive impact it has on our lives. Nothing can match or exceed the strength of our heart, the power of our mind, or the wisdom of our soul. Infants and toddlers generally amass endless toys from parents, family, and friends, hoping to keep them happy, occupied, and content for as long as possible. But no matter how expensive the toy, they may enjoy the wrapping paper even more than what is contained within. *i.e: Paula's doll !!*

⁓ We often disregard our most powerful gifts for the ones that seem to provide instant gratification.

As a child, our world was mysterious, undiscovered, and ours for the taking. Life was new and exciting, and it wasn't difficult to find even obscure objects to engage our interest. As we grew older, we quickly tired of the toys of childhood. As we headed toward adulthood, we swiftly discovered an entirely new realm of toys, some that played music, drove fast, or glimmered, sparkled, and shone as they vied for our attention. We are attracted to faraway places and to those things that we feel will provide us with the happiness and love we innately desire.

⁓ As we progress through life, we accumulate more and more "things" that we believe will offer us peace and happiness.

We are a society of consumption, based on the accumulation of things, possessions, baggage, in essence relatively pointless and meaningless items. As we mature, we realize that we have amassed an amazing quantity of items that we, inevitably, use less and less. The only value that these items continue to have in our lives is the value we place upon them. Before we are conscious of it, we have barricaded our life with the pettiness of this existence, pulling ourselves further and further away from the purity of our soul's purpose. As a society, we over-identify ourselves with our surroundings. We identify ourselves with our home(s), our cars, our clothes, our stuff, and even with the stuff of our children, friends, and family. We tend to over-identify ourselves with our work, to the point that when we retire or even take a short sabbatical, we are often unable to find peace.

We claim to be everything that we are not by identifying ourselves with those things that have no true relevance. When we eventually discover the terminal nature of life, we discern the paradox and parody of this gatherer-existence, realizing that we hold onto nothing but what we possess within. We are who we are, not in relation to our work or the things or people that surround us, but simply by virtue of the choices we make, our path, and our purpose.

> ⟿ We take with us only what is within our soul, and for others we leave only memories.

We are remembered by the trail we leave behind. At some point, we realize that we can no longer identify ourselves with what we have, for we are not our possessions. We are simply energy, as is our world and everything within it. The energy of thought is as powerful as the energy of motion, transformation, and strength. Our ability to affect positive change in and around our world is all that we have and all that we truly maintain.

> ⟿ We cannot identify ourselves with anything that exists outside of ourselves, for that is to identify ourselves with the external and not the internal.

As we continue to evolve, which quite often occurs at the bequest of aging or evolution, we shed our accoutrements. We become human beings of our own volition, finally free, living life to its fullest only through the connections we experience in this very moment. An entire lifetime is often required to understand the capitalistic trappings of society and the role it plays in supporting our continual consumption. But who we are is determined by who we choose to be in this moment and is a function of our soul and life purpose.

⟩⟩ Freedom is more than the ability to walk from place to place or to freely speak our mind. Freedom is setting our minds free.

Freedom is the peace of knowing that we are free spirits, not attached to the trite physicality of this existence. True freedom comes from using the tools and resources presented to us in order to experience life to its fullest, to share in its magnificence, and to follow our life purpose while giving to others so that they, too, may experience the greatness that is available to all of us.

Are We Truly Rich?

✳

He is a wise man who does not
grieve for the things which he has not,
but rejoices for those which he has.
—*Epictetus*

❧ Are we rich if we have a large amount of money?

❧ How much money do we need to be truly rich?

❧ Are we rich due to the number of houses we own or the number of "toys" we have at our disposal?

❧ Is there any way for money in and of itself to make us rich?

❧ Are we "rich" purely from our financial disposition?

SLEEPWALKERS. THAT IS WHAT WE ARE. MANY OF US LIVE A relatively shallow existence much of the time, with each day a reflection of the previous and no true destination in sight. Our country may be one of the economic superpowers of the world, but in reality we are a very poor society. We are poor in our ability to evolve and in our ability to serve. We are poor in our connection to source and to spirit. We are poor in respect to our personal contributions to others, in our appreciation of ourselves, and in acceptance of our own individuality. More than anything else, we are poor as a result of our inability to come into the fullness of ourselves as a function of our path and purpose in life.

୰ We are poor not due to our lack of possessions, but due to our lack of appreciation and fulfillment in any particular moment.

The richness of the universe is much greater than anything that can be earned or purchased in this world. This richness is a function of the possibilities within each and every one us and our ability to act upon our truth within every moment.

୰ We need to be wealthy in our giving to others and caring for ourselves. We need to be rich in our personal evolution and growth.

True wealth does not come in the form of money. Money has no real intrinsic meaning or value to anyone, for it is simply a tool used to obtain what we think we require within this physical existence. True wealth is our ability to find peace, connection, happiness, and love in every moment while following our passion and being of service to our community.

୰ Other than fulfilling our core physical needs, money does little in fulfilling us intellectually, emotionally, and most importantly, spiritually.

In our society, we are obsessed with our financial well-being. We can find innumerable resources rating the world's wealthiest people, the most successful companies, and the most powerful countries, but we might be hard-pressed to find a book that rates the happiest people in the world or the most fulfilled societies. How about a resource on the most selfless service-oriented cultures in the world or the people who follow their truth or who have found the deepest connection to their source? It doesn't exist because there isn't an external metric to define, analyze, or categorize our inner connection.

Collectively, by focusing on the wrong things, we put our attention into an area that provides the least amount of fulfillment. In order to evolve as a society, we must look beyond the trite accumulation of toys and physical possessions and look into our heart and soul, which is really where we live and breathe.

~ We must put our focus into our soul's truth and allow our own destinies to speak to us in every moment.

When we learn to listen to our own wisdom, we will discover that the metrics of this reality have no meaning whatsoever. The only metric that matters is the one within us, and even then only in comparison to our true path and purpose in life.

Having Enough

---◆◆---

He who is not content with what he has,
will not be content with what he doesn't have.
—Socrates

- Is it possible to ever have enough money or success?

- Do we ever have enough health, love, or connection to our source?

- Can we ever have enough time?

IN LIFE WE HAVE A DIFFICULT TIME OBTAINING ENOUGH OF anything. If we find success and even excess in one area of our life, we generally lack in one or more other areas. Beginning as children, we are taught a scarcity mentality around that which we desire: There isn't enough to go around; what we desire is difficult to obtain or in short supply. Our weekends are short and our evenings even shorter. Our paychecks don't last nearly as long as we would like, and success always feels like it's just over the next hill. At the end of the day, we are left with a deep-seated desire for more—more love, more companionship, more from our children, our family, and our friends. Invariably, what we actually desire is a deeper connection to our source.

↣ Everything we touch and feel, everything outside of ourselves, is limited in some way.

We are limited in the resources available to us on this planet and in the amount of time we are here physically in this lifetime. Our life is a reflection of this scarcity, and our solution to this dilemma is acceptance of who we are and what we have, to follow our life-path, to be eternally grateful, and to go within for what we truly desire. We don't know how much life we have left, but in this moment, we have the opportunity to be truly happy.

↣ We cannot obtain happiness; we can only *be* happy. We cannot obtain love; we can only *be* loving.

We cannot obtain more time in this life, for when our departure time comes, our ticket is non-refundable; our only choice is to be grateful for the time we have been allotted. The same can be said for being grateful for the money and physical items we have attained, the company we keep, and even the love and caring we experience. There are always people "worse" off than we are, people more challenged financially, emotionally, mentally, physically, or spiritually. Gratitude will take us further than we can imagine; the more we can appreciate, the more we will attain, whether in perception or actuality, and the greater our sense of peace and well-being.

↣ We have the opportunity to be happy and fulfilled in every aspect of our life. Scarcity is an illusion, for there is more than enough of all we desire and require in this lifetime.

Beyond our obsession with physical possessions, can we ever have enough connection to our source? Beyond what we determine to be success within this life, there is nothing more important than our connection to source. We can hoard money, climb the corporate ladder, purchase a large home, start a family, and have successful relationships, but it is our connection to our source that provides the eternal fulfillment that we long for. In truth, we can never have enough connection, for it is not something that can be stored or measured. However, by making the connection to our source a focal point of our existence, we have the opportunity for a profound and boundless connection to ourselves and to others.

⟩ What matters is the quality of the life we live in the time allotted.

Change

Why is it so hard to let go?

What are we afraid of?

Don't we realize that we need to let go of the past in order to move into the present?

Structure & Change

Nothing that is worth knowing can be taught.
—Oscar Wilder (1854–1900) Irish Writer

> ⊱ Why do we require structure?
>
> ⊱ What is "time" and why do we require it to manage every aspect of our reality?
>
> ⊱ Why do we box ourselves in, creating boundaries that leave little room for opportunity, connection, and evolution?

WE REQUIRE STRUCTURE, AND AS MUCH AS WE ADAPT AND evolve in response to change in our external world, we struggle when we find ourselves uprooted and unsettled. Yet we are required to modify our lifestyle in order to adapt to the world around us. Our daily lives are governed by structure, supported by balance, progression, and systems of evolution. As human beings living within a structured society, we have been programmed to live by the clock, to govern ourselves individually as a function of progress within our greater communities.

᜴ When we step outside of the box to free ourselves from the constrictions of a lifetime of systematic decision-making, we find ourselves addicted to the very structure we are trying to escape.

We are addicted to e-mail and the telephone, to pagers and day-timers, to alarm clocks and even the concept of time. These structures must be managed and controlled when they begin to stand in the way of our path and purpose in life and when they limit our ability to be fully present in the moment before us. Much like an addiction, we must slowly wean ourselves away from limiting structures and toward freedom. As simple as releasing this structure may seem, it is far more difficult than it sounds, for it is easier to bind than to free ourselves. Freedom requires a deep sense of commitment and a parallel understanding of the responsibility associated with such freedom.

The elimination of structure often goes against the flow of society and is contrary to everything we have been taught and observed over our lifetime. We are truly creatures of habit, and it is habit that helps to create the structure and eventual complacency within our lives. Change often takes time because we are beings of patterns, of rituals. Adaptation requires risk and, of course the opportunity for reward. We will choose to act and evolve only if the perceived opportunity exceeds the perceived risk.

᜴ We are the sum total of every decision we have made to this moment. If we don't like the results, we need to change.

As human beings, we are designed innately, genetically, and prepared intellectually to operate within certain patterns and systems, guaranteeing that every action does not require a conscious decision-making process. This response patterning becomes rote, allowing us to focus our energies on that which truly requires our greatness. When these autonomic responses become flawed or result in restrictive or undesirable outcomes, we are forced to reevaluate our patterns and change our behavior in order to obtain different results. In life, all solutions require this uprooting and restructuring of the patterns to which we have become so accustomed. Beyond physical freedom, letting go provides us with the opportunity to achieve the authentic, emotional, and spiritual freedom that is available to all of us.

Constant Change

I know well what I am fleeing from
but not what I am in search of.
—Michel de Montaigne

> ~ Why do we procrastinate in life?
>
> ~ Why do we wait to begin the activities that will positively affect and improve our life in this moment?
>
> ~ Why do we wait to make changes that will make positive and marked impact on those around us?

COMPANIES HAVE THE OPPORTUNITY TO BEGIN THEIR FISCAL year at any time of the year, yet we individuals wait until the New Year to affect any significant change upon our lives. Why not convert procrastination into a calendar event and take control of effecting change in our lives? What exactly are we waiting for?

~ Every moment is an opportunity for greatness, to make the changes that will bring us greater happiness and fulfillment.

We are not so individualized that one person's happiness has no affect upon another's. Our happiness will inevitably impact others, and the collective reality of the world in which we live is directly impacted by the happiness, fulfillment, and evolution of every one of us. As a society, we are often perceived as procrastinators, especially our younger generations. However, it is only the categorization of priorities that determines what we take responsibility for and what we allow to languish. Because we are limited in energy and time, we must make the choices that will maximize the positive results we seek in this moment. We focus on and allocate to that which is most pressing, most demanding, and that which stands before us.

୰ In order to find true happiness, we must recreate ourselves from the inside out, similarly prioritizing our life.

Many alterations seem minor in the moment but, nonetheless, can dramatically improve our life, often requiring only clarity of purpose and some follow-through. Sometimes it is the seemingly inconsequential aspirations that require the greatest amount of effort and provide us with the utmost opportunity for evolution. Other times, it is merely the commitment to action that sets into motion the positive change we desire.

୰ Positive and consistent effort will take us further than any momentary impulsive or reactionary outburst.

For example, physical fitness, health, and overall wellness are not one major event, but an ongoing commitment to caring for the physical aspect of our being. Knowledge is acquired over time, not through a whirlwind study session. Love and caring are not the result of one action, but develop from consistent actions over the course of our lifetime. Connection to our soul, to our source, requires the commitment and dedication of an entire lifetime. The formation of companies, the moving of mountains, and the creation of who we choose to be or become is the result of a lifetime of specific, consistent, and intentional action.

↣ Through conscious choice, we can take responsibility for our actions and not blame others or berate ourselves for not accomplishing what we were meant to achieve.

Just as there are no wrong answers, there are no wrong actions. Every step, every decision, and every action has brought us to this place, to this moment. Enlightenment and fulfillment can be ours as long as we follow our path and purpose in this moment and the one to come. We are here to positively contribute to ourselves and to others, and to take actions that are in our best interest, in those we love, and in our greater communities.

↣ Through conscious choice and ongoing evolution, we can become everything we desire. And in the end, we will know that we lived life to its fullest, did our very best in every moment, and became the person we chose to be.

Selection & Evolutionary Transition

We cannot put off living until we are ready ...
—José Ortega y Gasset

> ~ Why do we evolve at a different rate than those around us?
>
> ~ Why is it so difficult to find true friends with whom we can connect on all levels?
>
> ~ Why does the level of connection we experience with various members of our family vary on a day-to-day basis?

THERE IS NO COINCIDENCE TO THE LIFE-PATH WE HAVE CHOsen. Every aspect of our life works in perfect transparency with respect to the interrelatedness of our world. Even before we enter this world, we have made certain decisions about our life and the path we are here to experience. We have even chosen our family prior to our soul's entry as related to our life's purpose and the subsequent lessons that lie ahead for us and for them. At the same time, our family chooses us, and we enter a binding contract for this lifetime.

⁓ We make an "agreement" to be present for the opportunities before us, whatever they may be.

Not to belabor the obvious, but friendships are also two-way streets, naturally requiring the approval and commitment of both parties, existing and transforming in relation to our current place in life. As we continue to evolve, we frequently do so at a different pace than our friends and family. We continue to progress, one day reaching a conscious acceptance that perhaps we don't have as much in common with those around us as we once did. It becomes difficult to come together with these people, and when we do, it can be a trying, difficult, or even toxic encounter. If we aren't the ones being left behind in the evolutionary process, we end up trying to bring others along to where we are, working to educate, guide, and assist them. If they come along at all, they may come begrudgingly, or perhaps we realize that they are our connection to the past, and we must release them in order to move forward.

⁓ We may need to shed friends and family, temporarily or permanently, to make space for what we desire.

With each step in our evolutionary process, it may become increasingly difficult to encounter and connect with those whom we share common interests—geographically, professionally, spiritually—and a similarity of heart, mind, and soul. As we traverse life, overcoming the personal and collective mountains before us, we see a life of service is incomplete without being of service to our close and extended families.

From a spiritual perspective, when serving those we love, we can become frustrated with the immense difficulty of helping them work through their own immediate and ongoing challenges. Regardless of our effort or commitment, there are always family members who resist the journey or who are along superficially. Those we love the most are often the hardest to help. We may spend countless hours attempting to help them obtain the peace and sovereignty we have found, frequently enduring their endless struggles, coerced contemplation, and often the brunt of their eternal angst. We cannot trade them in, for they are our family in this lifetime. In the end, irrespective of their inability or unwillingness to change, we cannot relinquish our own path in life.

~ When we work on ourselves, our good example, perseverance, and connectedness can inspire others to discover their own respective paths.

Occasionally, spending time with our friends and family members can be draining, exhausting, or something that we tolerate rather than greet with enthusiasm. There is the risk that their rut may become our burden. Eventually we may perceive our relationship as less about sharing, support, and love, and more about oppression, conflict, and emotional upheaval. We may even momentarily harbor negative emotions such as anger or frustration, only to ultimately decide that we need to let go of trying to *fix* them, and simply focus on our relationship with those we love, fostering a healthy supportive connection. We must remember that their path is theirs alone, and although we can be of service, we can never take responsibility for their challenges.

In the end, we are all one on this great rollercoaster called life, but like everything else, we can only guide, recommend, and share. Many of us make major sacrifices in order to evolve, dedicating ourselves to persevering in the face of adversity. We invest ourselves entirely as active participants in this world. With that level of commitment, it is not uncommon to incite jealousy or feel like an outsider in the social circles in which we previously identified. Just as the opportunity for evolution is available to us, it is also attainable by everyone else, if only they are also willing to make the commitment and sacrifices required to obtain true happiness in life.

᷅ As we progress, we have the opportunity but not the obligation, to assist those around us in making their right choices.

Being of service does not mean that we need to subject ourselves to
another's pain or hardship. Instead, we must be ourselves, follow our
truth, do our part, and if absolutely necessary, create space and distance
from those who choose to disregard their truth and our assistance.
Everyone along our path plays a distinct role in our own evolution.
Our responsibility is to accept, support, and be of service to those in
our midst, and release those who stand in the way of our greatness—
only then will we fully comprehend the magnificence of this existence.

Simplicity

Why do we make life so complicated?

Can we simplify our lives?

Can we find balance through simplicity?

Keeping Life Simple

---◆◆ ◆◆---

Very little indeed is necessary for living a happy life.
—Marcus Aurelius

> ⤳ Why do we find it so difficult to find peace and harmony in our lives?
>
> ⤳ How do we simplify the reality we manifest for ourselves?
>
> ⤳ Why are we challenged with finding a reason for everything, a true purpose behind our reality?

SUFFERING IS OF OUR OWN CHOOSING; IT IS AN INTERNAL reaction to an external circumstance. History shows greater pain and suffering than we could imagine today, and even with our medical and technological advances, we still face the dawn as if we are all alone in our pain.

⤳ For thousands of years, humanity has dealt with the most difficult challenges, sorrows, fears, and hatred; and for thousands of years, humanity has prevailed.

Throughout history, for expansion of power or preservation of religion, cities have been built and destroyed; we have experienced mass genocide, civil and world wars, and a plethora of absolutely horrific acts. For selfish desires or religious prosperity, we have lived through the ravaging of villages, land, and people. Even in this "free" world within which we live, we find ourselves choking on or suppressing our feelings of anger until they are released upon trivial matters, such as a testy flight attendant, being overcharged at checkout, or even a pesky neighborhood cat. Such pettiness breeds even greater insecurity and uneasiness.

Beyond how we use our senses to perceive our world, our interpretation of the facts determines how we judge what appears before us. Our interpretation of reality is more important than reality itself, for reality itself does not exist without our interpretation. In anticipation of the future, our fears and concerns rarely extend beyond an internal emotional response to the fear of a potential outcome. Our fear of the potential future rarely compares to the inevitable positive outcome the universe has in store.

⭢ However, as the universe is in perfect equilibrium, pain and suffering are internal expressions of our outward perceptions, even though the outcome is inevitably positive.

Our commitment to a life of greatness forces us to face outward and inward challenges as we continue to evolve and follow our life-path. At times, the present moment may be a festering challenge, giving us the perception of a future of similar anguish, yet the long-term outcome will be desirable, for all events end positively, whether physically or spiritually. In every moment, our universe is balanced and eternally destined for a positive outcome, regardless of our perception and irrespective of the specific individual outcomes that are achieved. It is only our selfish, unfulfilled desires that breed internal anguish, even when the grand scheme of life results in eventual positivity regardless.

⊁ We can all benefit from the humbleness of a life of service and an openness to learn.

We can respect and empathize with those less fortunate, the minds and hearts of those who have lived through more hatred, violence, and death than we can ever imagine in all of our lifetimes. We can maintain the peaceful understanding that we will all transcend the physicality of this existence. Life is truly ironic, sometimes bestowing material prosperity on some suffering a poverty of the heart; other times afflicting hunger and homelessness on those strong of mind and fulfilled in love.

The reality of our world is difficult enough to comprehend in its own right, and we exacerbate the situation with our human tendency to overcomplicate all aspects of life and humanity. Again and again, we are challenged to balance being and reasoning, joy and sorry, prosperity and defeat. We manage these external challenges with our inner truth and commitment to our life-path and purpose. And again, we end in the same place as we began, in the space of love and fulfillment. Such is the path of the modern day human warrior—we wage a daily battle against the enemy of fear, hatred, and anger, the true enemies of the self. The greatest warriors, the most evolved, and the most powerful are those of us able to find inner peace, avoiding the tribulations of old. The modern day triumph is having the strength and power to become one with ourselves and to extend that strength to those around us.

⊁ Life grants everything to those who wait patiently in the space of love for moments of truth that give meaning to everything; but first we must have faith and take action.

Resolutions Year Round

—◆◆—

Why do you hasten to remove anything which hurts your eye,
while if something affects your soul
you postpone the cure until next year?
—Horace

> ↳ Why do we wait until New Year's to make resolutions that will, for the most part, be disregarded in short order?
>
> ↳ If we are seeking to improve aspects of our reality, why are we unable to follow through on our commitments?
>
> ↳ If we aren't going to follow through, why do we make resolutions at all?

THERE ARE TIMES WHEN WE ALL WISH WE COULD HAVE A NEW beginning, a fresh start, a second chance. However, the happiest people among us are those with no regrets, those who realize that while there may be experiences they wish had occurred differently or that were painful to endure, the ultimate outcome was a positive one. It would be nice if this lifetime were just a test drive, preparing us for the next life, the "real thing." Then we wouldn't have to take this one so seriously. There will always be situations we wish would have occurred differently or that we had experienced differently.

⁊ We must learn to accept that everything happens as it is meant to, thereby allowing us to move confidently in the direction of our dreams.

Because we lack the luxury of repeating any moment in time, why do we wait until the first of the year to make the changes meant to bring us happiness *now*? More than that, why do we take on those resolutions that we know will never see fruition? Why begin exercising in January when we know we will quit by February? We don't accept or consciously know that we will change course, but inside it is as though we are unable to commit to our own greatness. We all make the choices of greatest importance at our own pace. Rushed decisions may solve indecision, but if we are unprepared, they seldom make any difference in our actions except to expedite the eventual disappointment of a broken commitment. We set ourselves up for success by pacing ourselves and taking our lives on a moment-by-moment basis. We take control by making commitments that we are capable of achieving in this moment.

⁊ Taking responsibility for only that which we can control is really all we are able to do.

We cannot revile failure if we are unable to stay true to our own commitments. Commitments become even more difficult when we attempt to see them as lasting for our entire lifetime. We have a much greater chance of success when we take life on a moment-by-moment basis, committing ourselves to our own greatness and that of our communities. By committing to our own greatness, we can find compassion for ourselves, nurture our self-esteem, and support new beginning on all levels.

⁊ There are no mistakes in life, and there is no need to hold onto the past except in our memories and hearts.

There is also no reason to hold on to the future, attaching ourselves to a specific outcome, for that is a futile effort in any case. We have every reason to fully experience the present, because the present moment is the only element of time that actually exists. When we try to control or hold onto the present, it quickly becomes a frustration of the past. When we immerse ourselves within the present moment, fully enveloping ourselves in the reality before us, we have the opportunity to become one with ourselves and deeply connected to those around us.

Do Not Want

Nowhere can man find
a quieter or more untroubled retreat
than in his own soul.
—Marcus Aurelius

> ~ Why do we try to obtain happiness from others? Can another
> person actually provide us with what we truly desire?
>
> ~ Can we give or share our emotions with others so they can
> actually feel and almost experience them?
>
> ~ Can we actually be happy, even if only outside ourselves?

WHETHER NOW OR IN DUE TIME, WHAT WE RECEIVE FROM
others will never be sufficient for what we desire within, for fulfillment cannot come from anyone but ourselves.

~ Desire alone from another human being results in disappointment, regardless of intention or outcome.

If we receive what we desire from another, we may feel as though the other person has sacrificed on our behalf or that we have not given enough in return. If we are dependent on another for what we desire and do not receive it, we often feel let down, disappointed, or even undeserving. When it comes to desire that requires engagement from another, we cannot manifest against human will or human desire. As a result of the free will of the "human being," we are unable to manifest desire into our lives on the basis of what another human being chooses to do or not to do, or what another chooses to be or not to be in their life.

᙭ Our mental, physical, and emotional health is dependent upon ourselves individually, alone.

The spiritual path is to focus on ourselves, finding clarity around our personal belief system in order to obtain that which we truly desire. Other than our basic need for sustenance, it is the want or desire itself that requires the focus of our attention. If we can discover the root of our desire, we can strive to eliminate unnecessary outside influences that encourage unreasonable expectations in the fulfillment of our aspirations. All that we require is in abundant and available supply, but we need to take responsibility for the choices before us.

᙭ Each of us has the power to obtain whatever we desire—though all that we truly desire is within us.

There are always elements within relationships and in life that are dependent upon others, but it is our eternal freedom, balance, and peace that can come only from within. Relationships, desires, or needs that are primarily dependent upon others almost always result in failure, either from the other person becoming resentful for having to give in to our needs on a regular basis or from us being disappointed time and again by not getting what we want, when we want it.

᙭ In order to create the freedom that every one of us deserves, we must free ourselves from the dependencies of others.

We cannot depend on each other for the internal freedom and evolution we require. We must look within and find our freedom by trusting in spirit, taking the necessary actions, and letting go of all else. By trusting in this level of commitment, we release those around us to have the same level of freedom and internal intimacy that we require within ourselves for fulfillment, evolution, and freedom. We cannot depend upon others for what we personally desire, or we tie up our freedom on the whim of those around us. Beyond our core needs in life, we must find the strength within ourselves to make the choices that fulfill us.

~ Once we have satisfied our core needs, we must look inside for what we require for fulfillment in this life.

Physical freedom is very different from spiritual and emotional freedom. Spiritual and emotional freedom must be earned through conscious choice and intentional creation in each and every moment. Emotional freedom requires being true to ourselves, being vulnerable, being free to feel, think, share and connect from our heart and soul. Emotional freedom requires a commitment, dedication, and an openness and honestly toward life that is difficult to comprehend and even more challenging to live by. Spiritual freedom is reflected in our ability to listen to our truth and stay true to our path and purpose in life.

~ Spirituality freedom is making the choices in life that bring us true happiness and fulfillment.

Balance

What is balance?

Are we meant to be in balance?

Can balance be achieved?

Do we sacrifice too much?

Living in Balance

The unexamined life is not worth living.
—*Socrates*

> ~ What does it mean to live in balance?
>
> ~ Why is balance so elusive, a goal so paradoxical that we seem to obtain it only sporadically, even when in reality, obtainment exists only within our perception?

WE FIND BALANCE IN ONE MOMENT AND QUICKLY LOSE IT IN the next. Consistency and balance, striving for equilibrium and stability in all aspects of our lives, is what so many of us desire, but very few attain. Obtaining and maintaining balance is one of our greatest goals, which when obtained, impacts our overall well-being more than any other objective. In this physical existence, we are inundated every-day with chores, responsibilities, demands, and decisions. Having a proper balance in our everyday life provides an incredible opportunity for evolution and growth amid these constant stressors.

⤳ Some would say that balance is unattainable or unrealistic, but that opinion comes from those who underestimate our ability to experience peace within this moment.

Balance can reduce stress as long as the path to balance doesn't detract us from the greatness of the moment nor cause undue stress in and of itself. Balance will increase the quality and longevity of our existence, incorporating more of what is most important into our lives while allowing us to spend more time with those most precious to us. Overall, a balanced life provides the opportunity for an even greater experience of happiness and fulfillment in our moment-to-moment reality.

⤳ Living a life of balance is a constant, moment-by-moment integration of life's inner and outer priorities.

At its most basic level, a balanced life is simply an organization of priorities. At its most advanced and obscure, it is affecting change in space and time to contribute to and positively affect every moment. It is exercising kindness of heart in every communication and peace of mind in every thought. It is the unification of integrity, morals, and values into every decision and the sovereignty of the soul in every prayer. Most importantly, and at the core of everything, finding balance involves merging the realities of the present with the spirituality and love of our core. It is the entirety of ourselves invoked with every thought and in every moment throughout the day. It is the fullness of spirit within every breath, the vision we see through every blink of our eyes, and the love we feel through every beat of our heart. It is living for the moment and the accompanying lessons and glory within each one of them. It is simply who we are as human beings and why we are here.

⤳ You cannot "manage" your life, just as you cannot "manage" your diet; you can only live and you can only eat.

The act of doing is itself the only action that requires our attention. A bird does not *try* to eat, nor does it "administer" its offspring; it just is and it simply lives. We must also simply be. We cannot attempt to micromanage every aspect of our existence as if our success at multi-tasking were some sort of Holy Grail of optimum performance and the golden key to heaven's gate. Being present to the diversity of experiences and activities within our life is part of this existence, but being present in the moment before us, being "present for the present," is the true opportunity of this existence.

Living in balance is based on our ability to manage our priorities in a way that includes caring for ourselves and our loved ones, and offering our service to those we love and to those in need all around us. It is finding the time to do and be all that we desire in this lifetime.

⟤ Living in balance is our access to everything that we desire in life and beyond.

Life-Path & Poise

The best things in life aren't things.
—Art Buchwald

> ~ Where have we come from and where are we going?
>
> ~ Is a life of purpose a life of sacrifice? Do we sacrifice more than we should?
>
> ~ What does a life of balance actually look like? When do we know that we have achieved it?
>
> ~ Can we comprehend the dramatic shifts occurring in and around us?

AS EACH GENERATION PROGRESSES AT ITS OWN PACE AND IN its own time, the transitions that occur are evolutionary. Society's past generations have been immersed in the traumas of slavery, civil unrest, racial and gender inequality, and the transmutations of religion and relationship—many traumas that continue in some form today. In many ways, we have been forced to create dual-income families as a result of our inability to afford both the lifestyle necessary to provide for our children *and* the one we desire.

↬ We have been forced away from intrinsic balance and begun to experience the problems resulting from children receiving less quality family time from parents and other loved ones.

As we continue to seek balance, we see our societal attempt to rebound back to the center in order to rebuild the family dynamic. We strive for greater connection and more harmony. We aren't here to raise our children merely as subservient beings; they need to learn to think autonomously, to find their independence and truth, and to be of service in their own lives. It is our responsibility to act as role models and to be present for them when they require our guidance and leadership.

↬ No longer are we forced to choose our family over our work; we must choose work that allows us to be present for our families in addition to our spirituality.

We need to combine our career with our life-path such that we are constantly of service and compensated for such commitment. Instead of simply working to obtain what we require in life, we receive what we require by our commitment to serve. There is no right or wrong way to arrange our life, for it is unique to each of us. There are many ways to find the balance we inherently desire as we maintain sensitivity to the inner workings of our delicate family dynamic and interpersonal relationships. We create a lifestyle of balance by making conscious choices about work and being of service.

We must remember that we are always dependent upon others, for that is the entire dynamic of human existence. Given our capitalistic-focused society where we often work 60-, 70-, or 80-hours per week with nominal paid vacation days, is it any wonder our society is burning out? Should we be surprised that our quality of life with respect to our health, well-being, and time with our loved ones appears to be at an all time low? We have diseases that are directly attributed to the foods we choose to eat, ailments that we could avoid if we only valued our lives enough to respect our body for what it is.

〜 We sacrifice for the wrong reasons and for the wrong people, often seeking financial abundance at the sacrifice of our spirituality, our health, and our quality time with our family.

Abundance is a side effect of a life of service and balance. We can create a career of service that also satisfies our financial requirements. We must care for ourselves and our loved ones above and beyond the hedonistic callings of a life of physical promiscuity. We are provided with the guidance and direction we require to stay on course as long as we stay true to our life purpose and spiritual path.

Our Wisdom Sleep

———◆◆———

All men whilst they are awake are in one common world:
but each of them, when he is asleep, is in a world of his own.
—Plutarch

- ➤ Why do we take sleep for granted, as if it were some type of necessary evil?

- ➤ Why is sleep something we use to fill our free time?

- ➤ Why don't we set aside enough time for rejuvenation, healing, and rest?

SLEEPING IS THE TIME WE ALL REQUIRE TO CLEANSE, REJUVE-nate, and release. It is the time we let go and allow our physical, intellectual, emotional, and spiritual bodies time to release, facilitating the strength to continue. When we are young and need the energy required to grow, we sleep. When we are ill, we need sleep to rejuvenate. When we are elderly and we get tired, we sleep. Why do we assume that with the exorbitant stresses of our day-to-day lives, we can survive with minimal rest? Why do we assume that while we are nurturing our family, building our career, and attempting to maintain a healthy lifestyle, we can forego adequate rest?

 ⤳ It is not only our beauty that is compromised when we are sleep deprived, our wisdom, our intuitive power, and most importantly, our inner connection and bond with our source also suffer.

Some of our children's most important development, physical and otherwise, occurs during sleep. Why do we feel that as we age, we somehow require less and less rest for our own continually increasing levels of stress? As a society, we have a tendency to work ourselves to death—ironically, for the prospect of future freedom and rest. We commit to our marriage until death, but in many ways don't we have the same commitment to our work?

 ⤳ The guidance we require and our very best ideas come in their own time, but only when we remove ourselves from our daily chaos and honor ourselves with rest and rejuvenation.

We cannot force the answers we seek, for our soul operates along its own time continuum. We are but cogs in the wheel of eternal existence, and when the day is done, another will soon follow. We have a lifetime of days before us, and every morning we need to be well-rested and prepared for what the world has in store.

Just as we cannot approach our lives with an empty belly, we cannot expect greatness when we are exhausted, burned out, or short on the rejuvenation required to follow our life purpose and our souls' path to fulfillment and evolution. A life of greatness requires insight, energy, focus, and power. A life of purpose requires intelligent and intentional action in order that every moment is a reflection of everything we desire, everything we are. It is our ability to be, do, and become within the present moment that is our greatest opportunity.

∼ We must pace ourselves for greatness.

We must be compassionate and patient with ourselves, for we all have our "off" days. Just as we must be patient with others, we must be sympathetic to ourselves, for perfection is unattainable. Sometimes we will be crabby, tired, grouchy, or simply unemotional, and that is perfectly normal. Other days, it will be the ones we love who experience their challenges emotionally, spiritually, physically, or intellectually, and we need to support and provide space for them. We are active, energetic beings who not only adapt to our environment, but who also need time for recourse and recharge above and beyond the rest and rejuvenation we obtain in the evening hours.

We must take time to rest our body, for a rejuvenated body will support us in all areas of this physical experience. We must rest our mind, for the reward of a rested mind is vast and expansive, assisting us in making the right decisions and heading down the correct path. We must take time for our soul's guidance, as the wisdom we receive far outweighs any physical exertion of the moment. Without a deep and insightful connection to our soul, our efforts are futile, as we often exert ourselves in the wrong place, at the wrong time for the wrong reason, missing out on the true opportunities to be of service and follow our path.

∼ When we take time to rest and rejuvenate our entire being, we are rewarded many times over. Our truth, our purpose, and the answers we seek often come to us only when we stop to listen.

Slow Down

◆━◆

Forever is composed of nows.
—Emily Dickinson

◇ Why are we in such a hurry?

◇ Where are we going that time is of the essence?

◇ What is so important that it forces us to disregard the glory of the present moment and focus on a moment that has yet to come?

BEING A HUMAN BEING CAN BE EXHAUSTING, FOR IT TAXES the body, mind, and soul. Daily living can be especially difficult with the simple pressures and challenges of this physical world. There will always be another day, another time or place to do more, say more, be more, and achieve more, whether we are consciously a part of it or not.

◇ We need to pace ourselves, for each day we are granted the opportunity to begin again, to be the person we know ourselves to be, to act as we choose, and to manifest what we desire.

So many of us identify with what we do or what we have rather than with who we are. Although inaccurate, it is common for us to invest much of ourselves in our work, which ultimately becomes how we see ourselves. Unfortunately, our work persona often does not reflect the person we actually are or want to become, but merely who we choose to be in those particular moments. Most of us eventually evolve beyond our work, and when that happens, our work must evolve at the peril of restricting our own continued development.

ᔓ Life is not a casual sprint; if anything it is a marathon, with a clear finish line. We have only this moment in which to live, to be, and to appreciate—nothing more.

When we die, we simply finish this current phase of our physical manifestation, regardless of where we are in the universe's grand scheme. We cannot pace ourselves for death, as it is outside of our control. We can only pace ourselves for life and its allowance of time for continued growth and evolution, all of which are guaranteed to be part of our future in life or death.

ᔓ Every moment is simultaneously infinite and ultimate.

All the people, activities, and moments in our lives are merely constantly evolving pieces in the living puzzle of time and the continued personal and collective consciousness. We cannot rush the falling snow, trickling streams, or shifting mountains; nor can we rush ourselves, for there is a divine plan for all things great and small, on a schedule and timeline that is often entirely beyond our control. We must find our place within the vast network of opportunistic moments where things fall into place exactly as they are destined.

ᔓ Everything works out precisely according to the serendipitous reality of our universe, whether through our own conscious decision making or not.

Life Outside of Balance

The world we have created is a product of our thinking;
it cannot be changed without changing our thinking.
—Albert Einstein

~ Why is life often so chaotic, so stressful, and so overwhelming?

~ We know the definition of insanity, but is dramatic change is the only solution to our problems?

THE SEARCH FOR BALANCE IN OUR MATERIAL LIFE IS DAUNTING enough. But combine that with the eternal search for our personal life-purpose as part of the communal whole and the search seems practically impossible. In our chaos, we all look blissfully toward the days when we can retire, go fishing, spend endless hours with our children or grandchildren and quality time with our spouses, traveling to exotic places, or even finding time to read this book. We stress and strive every day, yet we seem keenly unaware of those around us who possess those minor accoutrements that might make our lives that much better.

~ We are unable to find balance *outside* of ourselves.

We get up early in the morning to go to work; we kiss our children goodbye while they sleep in their beds and drive past our neighbor loading up his boat to go fishing for the day. As true road warriors, we exhaustively travel for our work, sitting next to the family of four going to Europe for the summer. We say goodbye to our children as the bus takes them to school only to wonder if they are getting everything they require from us. We wonder how we are going to pay all of our bills while reading about the woman in Milwaukee who just won the Powerball Jackpot worth hundreds of millions of dollars. Our lives reflect everything that we see and experience.

ン We see that which we seek in everything and everyone around us—for they are merely reflections of our reality and our deep-seated desires.

Why are we obsessed with other people and their lives? Why are we obsessed with others' jobs, spouses, cars, travels, and experiences? Why do we spend more time talking about other's lives than looking honestly at our own? Why are we so quick to judge others and the choices they've made, often disregarding our own? Those who judge frequently do so to overcompensate for their own poor self-image, pitiful judgment, or inept decision-making.

ン Focusing on someone else's life is a poor excuse for disregarding our own.

We become frustrated in our lives, wanting so much more, yet unable to let go of what makes life so complicated and convoluted. We want all or nothing: We want a great career, a beautiful home and vacation home, money to travel, occasion to enjoy it, and time to serve others as part of our divine path and purpose in life. Alternatively, we want to let it all go, retire, be free, and do whatever we want.

Invariably, we set ourselves up for failure by living a lifestyle of excess that demands sacrifice—making choices that are contrary to what we truly desire. Everything in moderation is a balance we can all appreciate, for while the grass may be greener elsewhere, it still needs to be mowed, fertilized, and cared for.

Often what we think we need is dramatic, fundamental change in a new career, a significant amount of money, lots of free time, a new relationship, new friends, new hobbies, a new house, a ski condo, or an airplane. But what we really need is actually very minor, almost negligible, yet makes the most significant impact in our lives: Balance. It goes a long way toward helping us find the happiness we all seek. For many of us, letting go of everything seems fundamental, but very quickly we discover that such a dramatic shift in our external world requires an equally dramatic internal shift. Actually, the transition from structure to freedom, from hard work and effort to peace and trust, and from everything to nothingness is your choice to make.

~ The true transitions we seek are internal—for as our external environment is merely a reflection of our reality within, the balance, abundance, and fulfillment we seek is merely a shift in consciousness.

We can never be fulfilled externally, for there is never enough of anything in this world that can fill the void within our soul. We shift internally, create balance externally, and realize that what we need for happiness is minute and miniscule. We take a couple of days off to spend with our family; we commune with nature, change jobs if that is what balance requires, and we find the passion and purpose to make it all worthwhile. We take a long breath before speaking, set aside pockets of time for our loved ones, or even awake ten minutes early to commune with our soul.

~ In the end, it is the peace within that provides the fulfillment and balance we seek.

How We Live

Think positively about yourself . . . .
ask God who made you to keep on remaking you.
—Norman Vincent Peale

- Do we compare our life to others simply for the validation we require?

- Why is everyone else's life perceived as normal when compared to ours, or vice versa?

- Why does the grass seem greener on the other side?

DO WE REALLY NEED VALIDATION? DO WE NEED CONFIRMATION from the outside world that we are in the right place, doing the right thing? What is it about our external world that we feel is more accurate than our own inner compass? Can't our way be the right way? Can't our path be the right path? Why does it matter what anyone else thinks?

- We use others as the benchmark for a balanced and healthy lifestyle, and by looking outside ourselves, we will always find what we are lacking in our own life.

194

Looking outside our simple microcosm, we see a world with varied priorities, lifestyles, living standards, relationships, communication patterns, and of course, values. However, looking deeper, we see that everyone has his or her own individual challenges and opportunities for growth that manifest in their own methods and manners. Other less affluent cultures are often able to appreciate what they have and find happiness in every moment in a way that our society cannot. With all our physical possessions and the constant barrage of information invading every aspect of our world, we are often distracted from the very sensations and values that provide us with the meaning that we seek.

We look around and see other cultures and cannot understand or comprehend the way in which they live, perceiving many of their lifestyles and traditions as primitive, even bordering on inhumane. On the other hand, when other cultures look at our Western lifestyle and quality of life, they are just as confused. Even within our own little microcosm, a city dweller after speaking openly with a rural dweller or farmer, may quickly extend judgment about perceived desolation, isolation, separation, and boredom. Ask the denizen of the country to discuss the positive aspects of life in the city, and most are distraught and aghast at how people can even survive in such a horrendous environment. Each could make powerful arguments for their particular environment in contrast to the other's, and they would both be right. It is all perception and values.

> ⁓ How we perceive our own lives compared to that of another and the way we judge others in relation to ourselves says very little about the lives we lead; it only speaks about those we follow.

Where we live has nothing to do with how we live; but how we live is significant in relation to who we are or who we choose to be. At the end of the day, it is only the path we follow, the truth of our existence, and the connections we are blessed to make that create any relevance whatsoever. Regardless of our external environment and outside circumstances, we have the opportunity to find happiness and fulfillment in our lives in every moment. We can find our inner truth, within ourselves, right now.

———————————•◦—◦•———————————

Happiness

Can we ever be truly happy?

Can we be happy if we aren't healthy?

Is anything more important than happiness?

Where is the real joy in this life?

Is eternal happiness really possible?

Appreciate Ever-Present Beauty

Indeed, man wishes to be happy
even when he so lives as to make happiness impossible.
—St. Augustine

> ๛ Why do we struggle to find happiness?
>
> ๛ Is there a direct correlation between money and happiness?
>
> ๛ Why do other peoples' lives generally look superior to our own?

W E MUST TAKE TIME TO APPRECIATE THE BEAUTY OF THE moment, for surrounding every one of us at all times throughout our life is unimaginable and incomprehensible beauty. There is always something to be thankful and grateful for; it is only a matter of opening our eyes. As a society, we have become blind to the magnificence of our greater world, complacent in our comforts, and petty in our complaints. We quickly forget the reality of many of our brothers and sisters living on the street, in poverty, oppressed, or even facing imminent persecution.

~ We are trained to search for life's problems, the insecurities life inflicts on us, and its imperfections.

Most people would give anything for the abundance we are lucky enough to enjoy; yet at times, happiness evades even the most prosperous among us. Many of the world's poor live happier and more fulfilled lives to the extent that few of us can even comprehend. The grass always looks greener on the other side of the fence because we see it through our own filters and perceptions.

~ The perception we have of our own life will always be different from the perception others have of it.

We cannot control other people's perceptions of our life; we can only control the perceptions we maintain of ourselves. Our opportunity in life is to seek magnificence, to see and accept the beauty around us, and to appreciate all that we have been given and granted in this spectacular life. When our lives are less than we hoped they would be, we can merely look within and to our assumptions and perceptions to find the true limits of our happiness. Deep within each of us is the pure beauty that is free from judgment, existing regardless of outcome, and ever-present within every moment.

True Happiness

It is not easy to find happiness in ourselves,
and it is not possible to find it elsewhere.
—Agnes Repplier

- How can we be truly healthy if we are not happy?
- How can we measure success without measuring happiness?
- How can we follow the path to our truth when we are not happy?
- Is there anything in life more important, ultimately, than our own happiness and well-being?

We cannot be completely healthy unless we are sincerely happy, for true health encompasses our mental, emotional, and physical body. Happiness should be our greatest aspiration. Physical ailments will affect us all in due course, as will the disintegration of our minds, and the relinquishment of our memories. Within this physical reality, our best opportunity is to consciously choose happiness in all of its variations and manifestations. However, we cannot find happiness in and of itself, for it is a byproduct of a healthy and fulfilled existence.

〜 Happiness is all we can hope for; it is the most important aspect of our reality and the outcome of any successful experience.

Happiness is the answer to all things, but it is not a momentary or superficial happiness. Instead, it is a deep, soul-filling gratitude for the opportunity to serve. Genuine happiness is not an emotion or a feeling, but a sensation from our soul; it is being at peace with all things.

〜 True happiness is fulfillment from the inside out.

We perceive the happiness we desire as being around us, in our dreams of majestic places or when observing other people's lives that seem to be in greater harmony and filled with more happiness; but perceptions are misleading. True happiness is the end result of a life of service combined with a deep understanding of our path in life, and a strong inner connection to our source. Our life experience represents a quest for connection and companionship, especially because we are unable to "save" our current place in reality. Our ongoing life-education breeds continual opportunities to grow along our path to evolution and fulfillment, allowing us to connect more deeply to those around us.

Why do we get up in the morning? Waking up without a smile is a sure sign that our life is not all that we had hoped it would be. Happiness is at the core of what's missing in this world, a concept easy to understand in principle, but difficult to experience in our day-to-day lives. What does it take to find happiness in every moment? What foundation is required for a lifetime of happiness and fulfillment?

〜 Happiness can be momentary, but true and sustainable happiness requires fulfillment of our being, of our soul.

We can laugh and have a good time, but when the party is over, we require much more to maintain the type of high that makes us giddy with joy. Our respective paths can at times be fulfilling, but there are many other opportunities for happiness created by a spiritual sensation of achievement, of finding and following our path and purpose in life, of maintaining a strong connection to our source. Health on its own cannot bring happiness, but true happiness without emotional or spiritual health is not possible. Happiness becomes the hopeful end result of every fulfilled need. The Holy Grail, eternal youth, and life itself are all about happiness, which makes life itself so very simple.

Where is the eternal fulfillment we lust for? It cannot be found outside of ourselves, for the world is much too busy attempting to fulfill its own obligations to pay any attention to ours. What we desire in actuality is merely a sensation from within that allows us to trust, feel secure, fulfilled, and at peace. In essence, our external life allows us to find fulfillment and true happiness within ourselves. Happiness is not merely a smile or a laugh, but an overall sense of well-being, which is at the core of every personal goal. Our physical health eventually deteriorates, yet the ability to capitalize on and appreciate every moment has the opportunity to provide an abiding sense of happiness and fulfillment, regardless of who we are or our current stage of life.

⁓ No matter how long we live, happiness is the gauge of our ability to live fully in every moment.

Elusive Happiness

※ ※

Nothing is worth more than this day.
—Johann Wolfgang von Goethe

> ᚛ Why do we seek happiness?
>
> ᚛ Is happiness the most important element of our existence?
>
> ᚛ Why is happiness irreplaceable? Why can it not be replicated by any other sensation?

W HY DO WE OFTEN MANIFEST UNHAPPINESS BY PUTTING ourselves in miserable situations? Why do we have a hard time getting out of unhappy circumstances? Is happiness really so elusive?

Everyone seeks that certain happiness, that authentic sensation that cannot be filled outside of us—not by a big yacht, fancy cars, large houses, or even with other people through sex, intimacy, or connection. Happiness does not depend upon the world around us, although external events can contribute to our sense of well-being, our emotions, and our reactions. Happiness is a feeling, an emotion that exterior forces can impact but cannot control. Alternatively, it is also a major delimiter by which we analyze the moment-by-moment choices we make to determine if, in the end, we have created and experienced a fulfilled and joyful life.

～ While external factors can play an important role, the true happiness we seek resonates from within and expresses itself regardless of our external circumstances.

Happiness is anomalous. For it to be sincere, it must originate from within us regardless of our exterior circumstances. We pretend that happiness can come from medicine, mental health professionals, an extraordinary relationship, or other such outside stimulus; but that simply is not possible. A momentary spike of joy or temporary lapse of consciousness can give us the illusion of the happiness we seek, until the injection of delight has waned, and we are faced again with the reality of who we really are, and who we choose to be in this life. At times we can be shallow, pretending to reveal contentment or even manufactured cheerfulness, yet what often eludes us is sincerity. Others can see beyond this façade and directly into our soul as we expose the truth of our inner barometer.

～ We are restricted by what our internal reality will allow because we seek out the happiness in ourselves that we perceive or observe in others.

Every decision and emotion is predicated on some element of current or future happiness in our lives or in the lives of others. Happiness is a core factor of our being as we attempt to discover the reality of the world around us and our place in it. If we can follow our path while finding and sharing appreciation and joy, we will have achieved all that is available to us in this lifetime. As we work toward enlightenment, we learn that happiness is the cornerstone of balance and evolution.

⌁ Happiness is the hopeful outcome of every experience, yet is one of the few elements of reality that is entirely within our control.

Whatever is required for us to create true happiness and joy within our lives is worthwhile. We must allow this goal to give us the momentary courage required to make the challenging decisions essential to our individual greatness.

⌁ True and lasting happiness is the end result of a life of ongoing service, passion, and fulfillment.

The Power of Laughter

———❦❦———

*If I had no sense of humor,
I would long ago have committed suicide.
—Mahatma Gandhi*

⟋~ Why are we all so serious?

⟋~ Why do we take life so seriously?

⟋~ Why is it so difficult to find the joy, peace, and humor in life?

L AUGHTER IS ONE OF THE MOST POWERFUL HEALING MECHA-nisms available to us. We look for healing in all areas of our life and underestimate the simplicity of a smile, chuckle, or good-hearted belly laugh. Finding the humor in and around our existence allows us to soften our demeanor, loosen up, and appreciate the subtle coincidences of our existence. We can then find solace in the magic of the moment, the intricacies and oddities of our physical reality.

⟋~ Laughter can loosen up even the tensest among us, making the most stressful moments feel a little more manageable.

Laughter has the ability to release pressure and diminish the overwhelming nature of life like nothing else. We will always be overwhelmed and faced with obstacles that we perceive to be outside of our control. We will always be challenged to overcome situations that seem overwhelmingly consequential. Our life is continuously filled with opportunities for greatness, moments in which we have the ability to control and assume full responsibility. Our ability to overcome the obstacles that stand before us is a testament to our strength and resolve, our willpower and persistence, all of which can be handled with more fluidity and continuity when we are a little lighter, slightly softer, and a lot less tense.

Laughter is often exactly the medicine we require due the extreme nature of a given situation, for it is in those very moments when we let down our guard that we realize our situation could always be worse. We realize that we can and *will* get through any adversity; we concede that everything does work out in the end, somehow. If we are present for the moment, we can obtain the answers necessary to survive and overcome and appreciate the opportunities before us, for greatness is available to all of us within each and every moment.

⟞ Life is not as it appears at first glance, and it is our ability to see through the stress and perceived impossibilities that allow us to see the truth of our existence.

Default to a Smile

Man stands in his own shadow and wonders why it's dark.
—Zen Proverb

> ᴦ Why does it seem that most people walk around with a frown?
>
> ᴦ Don't all of us have so much to be grateful for?
>
> ᴦ Why does it take such energy to smile?

WITHOUT A PROGRAMMED ALTERNATIVE, WE OFTEN FIND ourselves walking around our offices, cities, and homes with constant frowns, exuding what appears to be a default expression of apparent depression or anger, sharing nothing of the fortunate lives we lead. Energetically, we share very little with those around us, as if protecting every ounce of energy so that those who gaze upon us will receive no information, no reflection, absolutely nothing. Why can't we smile, thereby saying: "Yes, I know life is incredibly difficult sometimes, but it is also truly fantastic"?

ᴦ Regardless of how we perceive our current situation, we all have much to be grateful for.

We never win when we compare ourselves to others. There are always those around us who seem wealthier, smarter, better looking, more successful, in better shape physically, or simply flat-out superior. As much as we pretend to be more than we are or have more than we actually do, the illusions we put forth will be mirrored by the world we perceive around us. But the temporary superiority or inferiority we feel is merely our perception, regardless of which side of the grass we are on. Our perceptions looking outside from within the bubble of our life are very different from those of the outside looking in. Simply put, we will never find peace or happiness by comparing ourselves to others.

➤ We can run from our life but we cannot hide. Regardless of the environment outside ourselves, we can be at peace.

We can all look inside for something truly remarkable in our life, about our day, or in regard to the amazing world in which we live. We can appreciate the magnificence of our reality smiling from deep within our soul, even if just for a moment, to share our passion and excitement with the world around us. Our smile is not an acceptance of the reality of our existence at face value, nor does it give credence to all of the negativity around us. Our smile merely demonstrates to others that regardless of our circumstances, we can find the positive elements within and around us. Smiling can change both our emotions and our physicality, for the simple act of smiling has a deep impact on our soul. Staying positive allows us to discover, experience, and appreciate the beauty and magnificence all around us.

➤ Our persona is perpetually changing, our very being altering with every thought and sensation.

Others perceive us based on our outward expression of what occurs within us. The subtle or unconscious thoughts of a restless mind are generally neither the most positive nor the most empowering, at least not until we can intentionally restructure our thinking process from one of pettiness and mediocrity to one of greatness and gratitude. There is much to be gained from staying positive.

⁓ Let us share the beauty of our life, express our glow, and open ourselves to connection with those around us.

Perhaps we can then take advantage of the opportunity to touch another's life in a miraculous way, assisting them in changing for the better. We can share ourselves with others, giving them the opening to step momentarily out of their worries, breathe in the light, and appreciate the moment they might previously have overlooked. In the process, perchance we will meet another remarkable soul with which to magnetize the glory and gratitude of our world, someone with whom to share our eternal and effervescent journey. There is so much for which to be grateful and appreciative. Let us share the beauty of this existence.

⁓ Even with an expression as simple as a smile, we can share our happiness and gratitude for life, for those we love, even for absolute strangers, and of course for ourselves.

Present Moment

Why do we obsess about yesterday?

Why do we wait for tomorrow?

Don't we realize that other than this moment, nothing else exists?

What is the difference between the present moment of today, and the present moment of tomorrow? Our world continues to move indifferently onward, with or without us.

In time, this too shall pass.

Only the Moment

No yesterdays are ever wasted
for those who give themselves to today.
—*Brendan Francis*

- ➤ Why is it so difficult for us to stop and appreciate the present moment, even if only for a single breath?

- ➤ When we desire happiness, why do we look to our memories to relive past moments of merriment?

- ➤ Why do we look to other generations for the freedom we desire or have missed?

AS CHILDREN, IT SEEMS THAT SUCCESS IS SET ASIDE FOR THE future when we will be free to act on our own volition, thereby allowing for the fulfillment of our every dream and desire. As we grow older, it seems that we look to the past for the happy memories of a time when we were free, when life was filled with an abundance of happiness, joy, and love.

In adulthood, the space between childhood and old age, it seems that there develops a disease of the mind that looks to the past for times of freedom from responsibility and to the future for financial autonomy, peace, tranquility, and the time to enjoy it all. This disease prevents us from being and experiencing not only the moment, but also the reality of who we are, where we are, and where we want to be. How did this disease encompass the human race, particularly the more affluent nations? How can we cure this undermining pattern that stands in the way of true happiness and fulfillment?

➤ We know that the only moment in time that truly exists is the present, for every memory was at one time the present, and every dream and desire has the ability to become the reality of the moment.

Between memories of the past, dreams of the future, and the chaos of the present, how can we truly enjoy the life we've been given? Memory is futile, for this moment, the present moment, holds all the answers we seek. Those with spectacular memories are quite often unable to focus fully in the moment, instead obsessing about time gone by. Some are blessed with a vision of the future, another distraction from the power of this very moment. We obsess about the past and exhaust the possibilities and potentialities for the future. In so doing, we miss the most precious opportunity available to any of us: the here and now. Memory is ingrained in the physical structure of our livelihood. Although it is intangible, and thus exists outside of our grasp, it becomes the basis for the reality we seek and a part of all that we desire.

➤ A life obsessed with memories is a life stuck in the past.

The lesson for us all is merely to slow down and realize that the present moment is all there is and all there ever will be. It is imperative that we fully appreciate the peaks and valleys of the current moment, for we will never have the opportunity to live this moment again. Appreciate all of it—the bickering, traffic, financial worries, family dilemmas, house repairs, body aches, work hassles, and the general politics of day-to-day living—as the opportunity to perceive and fully experience each moment. Of course, we must also appreciate the momentary smiles, sunshine, trees, hugs, laughs, love, accomplishments, peace, and the sense of fulfillment and happiness.

This information is not new; we all maintain generally dogmatic answers to most of life's unending questions, but knowledge has rarely been enough to entice us to make the appropriate decisions, even with the effort of conscious inquiry. We may receive the answers to our questions, but if the answers are not giving us what we require, are we really asking the right questions?

⌥ It is always more difficult to live as the eternal optimist, fulfilled in love and happiness, than it is to live its alternative of eternal negativity, loneliness, and turmoil.

The continuum of time is never as linear as we imagine, for it is an obscure metric that does not actually exist. Time is a construct, an attempt to measure our personal reality. There really is no time continuum. We have this precise moment and nothing more. The past exists only in memory, and the future exists only as prediction, thought, concept, or merely a recreation of history. Ironically, we traverse our own realty, struggling to have "enough time" and complaining that we just "don't have time!" In truth, we are absolutely correct; there is no such thing as time.

⌥ We have precious few moments to give, share, and connect.

We can never relive a moment except in memory or by futilely attempting to alter our reality of the past from the present. As a society, we are obsessed with time, particularly because we are fixated with that which is outside our control. Our entire communal reality is based on the belief that everything has some element of control, if we can find it. We are trained and educated to develop our own level of structure and control, whether over our lives, our work, or even our relationship with other people. Consider global phenomena such as nature, the atmosphere, societal tendencies, disease, and the creation of the universe itself. We spend billions of dollars and tremendous amounts of time and other resources attempting to understand, explain, and eventually control that which appears to be outside of ourselves.

꩜ We must accept what we cannot control and exert the greatest influence over that which we can, for that is the only way to take responsibility for the greatness of the moment and find true happiness and fulfillment.

We must appreciate this moment, for we will never have the opportunity to recreate this exact moment again.

Trust the Moment

———— ◆◆ ◆◆ ————

Happiness is something final and complete in itself,
as being the aim and end of practical activities whatever . . .
Happiness then we define as the active exercise of the mind
in conformity with perfect goodness or virtue.
—Aristotle

⟿ How do we prioritize the many elements of our existence?

⟿ What is the most important element of life?

⟿ Why are we searching for meaning? Why does it appear so elusive?

⟿ Why do we laugh at the challenges of yesterday, worry about the challenges of tomorrow, all the while struggling with the challenges of today?

WE SPEND OUR ENTIRE LIFE SEARCHING FOR MEANING IN ALL things, for the path of greatest importance. We try to figure it all out, but in the process we exhaust the short time available to experience the truth and beauty within each and every moment. We are caught up in the concept of obtaining *things*, expecting to find success through fruitless acquisition. Our external lives are filled with pressure, demands, and the attempt to find fulfillment through what appears to be realization of our needs and desires. We all enter this existence as a fragile being, and we all will physically die in a similar manner—but it is only the filling, the intermezzo, that separates us from one another.

~ We all seem to have the answers for everyone else's life, but rarely for our own.

We are never short of an opinion for those we care about and even for those we don't. We are never too slow to judge, criticize, or question others, and in so doing we actually showcase our own judgment, criticism, and questioning of ourselves. We see our world as a reflection of how we see ourselves, for our eyes are the filters through which we perceive the world. Our belief system becomes our inner compass, the baseline for how we see our world, created as a function of our childhood education, all of our experiences and interactions, and who we are and who we choose to be.

We govern ourselves through an individualized justice system managed and overseen by constitutional law. We make choices for ourselves and judgments of others based on what we perceive to be *right* and *wrong*. We essentially create boundaries for ourselves within which we coexist with one another. Outside of these boundaries, we jeopardize the little peace and prosperity we *do* achieve by questioning our own motives and abilities and whether we deserve the fruits of our efforts. We awake to the stresses of our life, our family, and the chaotic world in which we live. We try to make our life and our world better for generations to come.

In the end, we may not be able to make our world a better one for future generations, but it will most assuredly be a different one. They will have their own version of the same challenges and opportunities we experienced, and the only thing we can provide them is our guidance and perhaps some tools they can use to better govern their lives.

↣ We would all take life a little less seriously if we validated our truth and had certainty in our beliefs.

If we were able to fully trust ourselves and our inner truth, we could valiantly commit to those things that would make all the difference. If we knew that success was guaranteed, would that give us the strength to commit to the opportunities before us? If we knew we could not fail as long as we followed our path and our truth, would that grant us the power to succeed? If we live every moment in the firm knowledge of who we are and what we are meant to achieve in this life, rather than living in trepidation, what kind of life would we have? What would our world look like? What kind of world would we leave for our children?

↣ The most difficult decisions of today are often fodder for tomorrow's laughter.

Our relative perceptions tend to cause the extreme stress, conflict, and contemplation of the moment, often manifesting physically as heart attacks, pain, suffering, and even death. We must trust, stay focused, and maintain full engagement in this world. We cannot run away. We are all an intricate part of our global community, each of us with an essential role to play.

↣ We have all come here for a reason, and our only assignment is to remember why and to live our truth in this moment, for it is the only one that exists.

Desire of the Moment

People wish to be settled:
only as far as they are unsettled is there any hope for them.
—Ralph Waldo Emerson

> ~ Why are we all in such a hurry despite our best efforts to slow down?
>
> ~ Why do we try to fill every free moment with activity?
>
> ~ Why do we all struggle to slow down enough to fully appreciate the moment at hand?

WE ARE ALL *TRYING* TO WIND DOWN OUR LIVES IN SOME FORM or fashion in an attempt to find more quality time for our families and friends, for ourselves and our *own* spirituality. We look to our elder years as the time when we will inevitably attempt to remove chaos from our lives, slowing down to appreciate the moments at hand.

~ The ultimate paradox of our lives is that we are all trying to accomplish more in less time in order to obtain more free time, which we often use to do even less.

Doesn't this scenario sound absolutely ridiculous? During our free time, we try to squeeze into our life as much activity as possible, whether on recreational activities outdoors or inside fixing our homes, watching television, working out, or reading. We are always trying to do more of whatever it is we are doing, whenever it is we are doing it.

During our off time, we have lists of errands to run, whether for our children or for ourselves. We try to squeeze in time to connect with our friends, read the paper, take a nap, clean the house, or take a hike. We don't seem to have ample time to exercise, to finally read that book we bought last month, to connect with old friends or extended family, or even to sit and enjoy the moment. We think that when we retire or when our children are older, we will have time to take care of ourselves, but in truth that is seldom the case. Our priorities change, our needs change, and the environment changes. We live in a time of constant evolution, and our life generally reflects the chaos in which we live.

᠊᠊ If we are unable to find the peace and magnificence we desire within this moment, it is unlikely that we will find it in the one to come.

The reality is that we do not achieve greater spirituality merely by quitting our jobs or going to church. And we do not become better parents just by taking more time off, although in many cases it does help. We become better human beings by the manner in which we handle the day-to-day chaos of our lives, by the choices we make in every moment. We become better parents by being present for our children when they are with us and by making our best effort to be there for them when they are not. We become better children by being available to our own parents while they are still alive and we are able to be part of their lives. We become better people by slowing down enough in the day-to-day moment to be fully present for the opportunities before us.

⁓ We become who we are in every moment of every day throughout the course of life, rather than when the world around us suddenly stops.

How we handle stress, exertion, exhaustion, havoc, chaos, problems, success, abundance, and peace define our character. Life does not wind up or down; it is merely our perception of it that changes with every passing moment and how we choose to experience that which is available to us. Everyone can be peaceful and contented on a beautiful Sunday morning while reading the paper on the porch of a country cottage. We need to bring that magnificence, inspiration, peace, and contentment to our workplace, our community, our neighborhood, our family, and our friends, giving us the opportunity to become the person we desire within our world. We are seekers. And from the perspective of our higher consciousness, we all have the same resources available to assist us along our path. Instead of working to find time for ourselves, we need to find ourselves in everything we do, and we will be fulfilled and content as a result.

⁓ True happiness, peace, fulfillment, and success are found in the current moment, irrespective of the past or future.

Setting Boundaries

—◆◆—◆◆—

We are always getting ready to live but never living.
—Ralph Waldo Emerson

⟩~ When the phone rings, do we always answer it? Why do we always answer the door?

⟩~ Why have we become so dependent upon one another that we must be available 24/7? Are we that important?

⟩~ Do we have any real boundaries?

⟩~ When we call people, why do we become upset when they don't answer the phone or when they don't call us back right away?

JUST AS LAWS ARE DESIGNED TO BE TESTED, WE SET BOUNDAR-
ies for our children to push against and eventually break. We naturally require the same type of structure for ourselves. We tend to seek
out for our own best interest, requesting time, energy, and resources
from others. Generally, our selfishness is not a result of disrespect or

animosity, but in order to care for others, we must first be able to care for ourselves.

~ We are continually faced with the chore of implementing boundaries for ourselves and those around us in order to protect our own resources.

We can be a part of our greater community while simultaneously and politely declining those tasks or requests that have the potential to push us over the edge. We all have needs and desires, and as we move through life as part of a community, we depend upon others to assist us along our path. When we connect and interchange in a co-dependent society such as this one, we must realize that as we rely on others, we eventually become dependent upon them, and vice versa.

~ Boundaries are required to keep all of us on task and on target.

To a degree, we have become a society without boundaries. Physically, in metropolitan areas we live on top of one another. Emotionally, we make ourselves accessible at all times through cell phones, text messaging, and e-mail, all the while expecting our family and friends to do the same in return. Not surprisingly, we find it increasingly difficult to create a healthy distance from our world in order to nurture the essential connection we require within ourselves. The interruptions of a life that is "always on" eventually leads to burnout, exhaustion, frustration, and even disease. We are part of a society where no other activity seems more important than the one that disrupts the present moment, either via the telephone, e-mail, or even the front door.

Do we really have to answer the phone every time it rings? Is it more important to field an interruption from the outside world than to connect with our spouse or child? Why is it rude to interrupt two people engrossed in conversation, but a cell phone that rings during an interpersonal conversation will be acknowledged and even answered? We know how we feel and perform after restless nights of constant interruption, but what happens to a life continually interrupted and distracted from path and purpose? As part of setting boundaries, we must also realize that it is alright to have uninterrupted time, to separate ourselves from incoming activity and the outside world, and to take the time necessary to connect with our loved one, or ourselves.

↗ Sometimes we need to turn off our external stimuli in order to turn on the connection we require to our higher self, to our soul.

Staying fully present with the connection before us is the true opportunity of this lifetime, for our inability to connect directly often precludes us from connecting at all. The moment at hand is the only one that truly exists, and it is the only one that maintains the opportunity for service and connection.

Immediacy & Contemplation

It is folly for a man to pray to the gods
for that which he has the power to obtain by himself.
—*Epicurus*

> ⁓ Why do we live in a society that requires instantaneous response in every aspect of our lives?
>
> ⁓ Can we really create a high quality of life if we demand such immediacy?
>
> ⁓ Do we really need answers to all of our questions RIGHT NOW?

WE REQUIRE IMMEDIACY IN ALL THINGS, WHETHER BY request, demand, or simply Mother Nature. We have lost the ability of patience and as a result, have lost the ability to connect with spirit for the wisdom we seek. We put ourselves in difficult situations because of our inability to stop long enough to reflect and to contemplate the full reality of every moment. We pressure those around us to provide us with the exact answer we require at the exact moment we require them.

~ Do you know what time it is? Do you know how to get to Central and University? Two lattes and a croissant, please! Can I do this, can I do that, do you mind if, how about … etc., etc.

We look for approval, we seek forgiveness, and yet we want answers right now, expecting immediacy in every response. In the end, everything we require and most of what we desire is within this physical world, yet it is spirit to whom we direct our demands, expecting immediacy to all of life's perceived inconsistencies.

~ For the answers that allow us to progress along our path, we must merely pause and accept a momentary lapse of consciousness in order to step out of our mind and connect with the infinite.

By stopping to breathe and let our soul run its course, we invite spirit into the moment in order to help guide us. We expect much out of our guiding spirit, but in the exact moment the guidance is available to us, we often allow our ego and mind to take control, backing us into a corner and putting us into a no-win situation. We talk ourselves out of our truth, resting safely within the limitations, fears, and restrictions of this physical existence. When we are able to reconnect with our higher self, with our true spirit, we are able to obtain the guidance we seek.

~ From gratitude to acceptance without judgment, we create new opportunities from which to learn, adapt, and evolve.

At times, we are such simple people, often unable to even comprehend that which is presented before us. We ask for guidance and when it arrives, we refuse to believe the messenger or in the method or manner of delivery, thereby discrediting what we receive. We are critical and judgmental. We are always looking for a reason not to believe in what is given to us. Why does it matter who delivers the message?

~ The guidance we seek is not going to arrive in the sensation-alized, spectacular, and often overly dramatized storybook fashion.

The Red Sea is not going to part, and we aren't going to find the Ten Commandments buried in the mountains. The guidance we seek will return to us in the form and fashion of our current life. We receive our guidance and our answers as a reflection of the reality within which we live. But we are often unlikely to believe, understand, and accept them because they appear "too close to home."

We suffer from the "burning bush syndrome." We yearn for a higher being or power to show itself to us and provide us with an exact, detailed, yet simple and easy to follow plan to help us. We want specific details, including expectations, preparations, and outcome. Instead, we receive an infinitely subtle message, so abstract as to elude even the most conscientious listener. We purchase gasoline for our less than efficient automobile and while so doing, overhear a mother screaming at her children. In the midst of our eavesdropping, we hear a word that reminds us of someone from our past, and suddenly we make endless connections in our mind pointing us to the answer we have been asking for.

~ We must be able to distract ourselves *from* ourselves long enough to connect to our source, to our truth, and access the power of the universe.

We cannot always rationalize our thoughts, nor can we fully understand the intricacies of our decision-making process or the beliefs or reasoning behind the choices we make. At a glance, we often present ourselves as schizophrenics or psychopaths looking for meaning within our warped realities, utilizing our own unique methods and manners that are increasingly hard to conceptualize. We rationalize our actions and existence as only human beings can, maintaining a wide range of beliefs, feelings, and ideas that act as the baseline for our decision-making and our reality. We attempt to connect the subtle inconsistencies of our lives in order to find the very meaning we seek. We need to take a breath, pause, reflect, and appreciate the moment in order to receive the very wisdom we so desperately desire. We need not seek out nor overanalyze that which is presented distinctly before us.

~ We must trust that the wisdom we require and desire is available to all of us all the time, without hierarchy, priority, or delay.

Peace

How do we find peace?

Where do we find it?

What does it look like?

Once we find it, can we hold onto it?

Finding Peace in Chaos

——◆◆——

*I cannot imagine how the clockwork of the universe
can exist without a clockmaker.*
—Voltaire

- ~ What exactly is peace? How do we find it? Where do we look?

- ~ Do we need external peace to find internal peace, or is it the other way around?

- ~ Can life be trouble-free? Can we find paradise on earth?

IT IS EXTREMELY DIFFICULT TO FIND PEACE ON THE INSIDE IF there is no peace on the outside. As we try to center ourselves, regardless of the outside circumstances in which we find ourselves, we are often challenged by what we perceive as some of the most intricate, complex, and difficult events in our lives. Finding peace when life is simple is no evolutionary activity. We all excel when life is easy, uncomplicated, and trouble-free. The solution is to view all aspects of our lives as deviations from our inherent simplicity, giving us the opportunity to overcome the obstacles before us with effortless ease. Many times the perceived "overload" is far more detrimental than the process of resolution. We are often forced to face the obstacles to which we are destined to interact. The resulting opportunity is to see the greatness and simplicity of our manifest reality and how our life-path unfolds within it.

⁓ If we have peace within, we can find peace without.

Sometimes we cannot immediately change the chaos around us and are forced to live for awhile in it. We can, however, change our experience from utter chaos to focused intention. This will help us to see the forest for the trees so we can make decisions based on truth, not assumptions. We can then better filter the external reality through our inner clarity, distinction, and peace.

⁓ We must find ways to alter our external environments in order to give ourselves the opportunity to find peace within.

Ideological paradise is typically a kind of isolation. External paradise is associated with quiet beaches, secluded islands, crystal clear ocean water, lush forests, and any other aspect of our physical environment that includes privacy and peace. When we think of paradise, why don't we think of a family reunion, a staff meeting, or taking the subway in order to connect with those of like-mind? Instead, we run away from the hustle and bustle of life to find the peace and serenity we require. As our society continues to expand at an exponential rate, the true physical paradise we seek becomes farther away and harder to find. We are continually forced to find the seclusion and tranquility we desire from within ourselves. Nobody can provide for us that which our hearts truly desire.

⁓ Everything that happens to us happens within us.

We experience on the emotional, spiritual, and physical plane, but what we experience happens from within us, from within our soul. We have the ability to accept or reject and to adapt to what we experience in our world. Ultimately, it is our soul that sustains us and allows for the evolution of our being. The outside world is nothing; it simply does not exist without our acceptance of it.

⌇ The external nature of life is nothing without the internal nature, the perception, and the actualization of experience.

If Knowledge Were Enough

The only person you should ever compete with is yourself.
You can't hope for a fairer match.
—Todd Ruthman

> ~ Why aren't the smartest people in the world also the happiest, richest, or most successful?
>
> ~ Why aren't those with the greatest intelligence or the most extensive education also the most satisfied?

KNOWLEDGE IS NEVER ENOUGH. WE ALSO NEED WISDOM AND intelligence. Although we may know what we should do for the health and wellness of our body, our mind, and our soul, we are unable to execute accordingly. We fully understand what we should and should not ingest, but this knowledge does not provide us with the motivation to actually change our ways or make the right decisions. Memorizing sports statistics, historical events, or even every aspect of our political system is not enough to change the path of our existence. Reading and understanding everything in this book is not enough to create either a fulfilled or an evolved existence because we need to successfully utilize the relevant and appropriate knowledge.

~ Knowledge is not enough to become who we choose to be within this lifetime.

Our future is predicated upon what we conclude and act upon in this very moment. We are often limited by our own interpretation of our past or by who we *think* we are, but these things are irrelevant in respect to who we *choose* to be. How can we determine who we are with the faculty of our mind alone? We cannot self-analyze, so to speak, using our mental factors to reflect upon ourselves. We are also unable to trust the views of others, for they offer a reflection through the filter of their own biases. Our only option is to reflect upon ourselves not in a comparison to those around us, but rather as a reflection of who we are in the present moment versus who we were in the previous one—who we are now versus who we choose to be. We look at ourselves and determine whether or not we meet our own objectives, and if we have evolved.

~ We compete only with ourselves, and the true determinant of success in this existence is how we evolve on a moment-by-moment basis.

Knowledge is simply the understanding of the systematic structure of our existence and how we move forward in the evolution of ourselves individually and communally. Yet maintaining the knowledge of our existence is not enough to overcome the limits of our past, our mental state, and our existence. Evolution requires an unfettered belief combined with a commitment to action. Our world is how we choose it to be, but not as a function of what we know or what we experience. Our world is our world because of our belief system combined with our knowledge base; and in turn, these elements become the determining factors for the actions we take.

⟿ No amount of knowledge or understanding is enough to change the course of our existence personally or communally.

Through conscious choice, we can structurally transition our existence, allowing for our evolution and continual adaptation toward the life that we desire, the life that we deserve.

⟿ Wisdom comes from the successful application of appropriate knowledge.

Peace of Mind

———— ❦ ❦ ————

But what is happiness
except the simple harmony
between a man and the life he leads?
—Albert Camus

> ⁓ Why is it so difficult to find balance in every area of our life?
>
> ⁓ Why does it seem that as soon as we find balance in one area, we lose it in another?
>
> ⁓ How do we prioritize?
>
> ⁓ Do we need to find internal peace and obtain personal health in order to have true happiness?

THE ABILITY TO WAKE UP IN THE MORNING AND ACCEPT, understand, and appreciate everything before us is much more than the acknowledgment of the physical plane as it is presented to us. Impeccable balance within every area of our life becomes the ultimate challenge as we manage our moment-by-moment reality. We cannot find true peace if we have balance in some areas and utter imbalance in others. While attempting to find peace of mind, we need to start with those things that most greatly impact our lives.

We are dependent upon the reality we form, accept, and manage for every aspect of our understanding. It is not so daunting that we need to solve every problem, but we need to face and handle the challenges that stand in the way of our greatness and our happiness, especially the ones we have a tendency to avoid. Peace comes with balance. Some people will tell you that balance is not attainable, and it isn't if you are looking for an equal amount of time in every priority.

~ Balance is not perfect equilibrium. Balance is perfection in disequilibrium; it is simply prioritizing time to find the beauty, gratitude, and greatness in every moment.

Eternal balance in life requires making the difficult decisions, having the tough conversations, and making the life alterations required todesign our lives consciously and in exactly the manner we desire. Life will happen outside of our plan, but it is our ability to place intention upon that which is within our control that gives us the greatest opportunity for balance and peace. We must set boundaries. They must be cognizant of our limitations as well as our desires and life purpose. Finding peace requires actualizing balance in every area of our life.

~ As our external environment is merely a reflection of the internal, beyond the alterations of our physical reality, we must focus within for the balance and peace we seek.

If we cannot find peace, we will not have true happiness. If we cannot find peace, we will not have health. If we cannot find peace within ourselves, we will not evolve to the fullness of our being. We will struggle not only with the gift of life but also with our true opportunity to serve. Finding peace appears more complicated than it really is, for peace can be found in every moment, all interactions, and in each nook and cranny of our existence because it is the underpinning of everything.

⌇ Peace is our connection to soul, spirit, and the truth within.

Peace is the destiny afforded to all, regardless of the external world at large. Peace exists regardless of race, genetic disposition, affluence, and karma. All that we desire and require is available to us if only we have the courage to choose it. We all have the opportunity to find peace in everything we do, regardless of how we perceive or experience our world.

⌇ Focusing on our inner connection and bond to spirit will help us make the decisions that will allow us to find balance and the peace we desire.

Creating Space for Retreat

Nowhere can man find a quieter or more untroubled retreat
than in his own soul.
—Marcus Aurelius

> ๛ Why do we need a break from our life?
>
> ๛ Why do we feel the need to get away from the life we have created?
>
> ๛ Where and how can we find peace within the frequent chaos of our existence?

WE ALL NEED TO GET AWAY FROM OUR LIVES FROM TIME TO time, vacation from our work, family, friends, communities, and from our own reality and selves. The show will go on, but sometimes it must continue without our unwavering contribution. Sometimes we need to walk away from our life in order to reflect upon the truth of our existence. We need only look inside to find true peace and a respite from life when seeking the space required for rejuvenation and regeneration. Often though, going inside while surrounded by chaos is extremely challenging. It is difficult to sit in a quiet and relaxed meditative state while surrounded by the challenges of our existence. So we must alter our external environment in order to assist with our own internal adaptation and evolution.

~ We evolve from the inside out, and by consciously altering our environment, we give ourselves the opportunity to create a new pattern for ourselves to explore.

From time to time we all require a certain space to maintain healthy and balanced lives. The liberty we require may take the form of anything that brings us momentary peace and security, and for each of us, it may be something entirely different. It could be canoeing on a lake, watching a football game, running away to a secluded mountain cabin, or simply going to a special place from our childhood. It could involve a childhood experience, such as eating pancakes or cereal. Or it could be as simple as a morning walk around the neighborhood. Creating space can be as effortless as sitting in front of the fireplace or on a park bench after work to gather our thoughts and then to let them go.

The simple truth is that we all require respite in one form or another. Many of us have a serene segment of time built into our daily schedule, whether it is our morning commute, a bus ride, or the extended shower we take much to the dismay of our housemates. For the health and sanctity of our being, we require this space not only from the perspective of recharging our batteries, but also in tribute to our life and in respect for our family and community.

~ We require peace not only within our world at large, but most importantly, within ourselves.

Creating Emptiness

When your inner and outer energies radiate in harmony,
you are blessed and spiritually magnetic.
—Jasmine Heiler

> ⤳ How do we create space in life for what is to come?
>
> ⤳ If we live as a factor of the past, how do we make room for the future?
>
> ⤳ Why do we become so attached to physical *things* that we are unable to let them go?

WHEN THERE IS EMPTINESS IN LIFE, THERE IS SPACE FOR what is to come—for the unknown and for the fulfillment of our dreams and desires. When we are full, we can accept no more. When we are empty on the outside, we are free to discover, to travel, to explore. When we are empty or unfulfilled on the inside, there is space to *become,* for new information to enter, for learning and acceptance. We all must learn to create space within and without, to stay open for the unexpected and unpredictable. We make space and in so doing make ourselves available to the unknown, the unpredictable, and the future, which provide the greatest opportunities for evolution and transformation.

⟫ Creating emptiness requires letting go of what we hold near and dear to our ego, making space for what we latch on to with our heart and soul.

In the end, most of us would be happier if suddenly, many of our worldly physical belongings merely disappeared. It would force us to let go, become detached, and make ourselves available to appreciate what is most important in our lives. The alternative is to live with attachment and obsession, constricted by the physicality of this world. A mentality of scarcity rarely allows for our fulfillment, especially when the mere thought of letting go of our possessions causes heartache, grief, and despair. By holding on too tightly onto anything, we constrict the flow of energy. This restriction results in an even stronger grasp on what we are afraid of letting go and, consequently, even smaller openings to attract all that is available to us, all that we really desire. Our entire world exists in perfect equilibrium and is designed for all things to flow continuously.

⟫ When we let go of what stands in our way and send undesired energy away, we create space to attract what we desire.

There are those who are willing to sacrifice everything to achieve their dreams, putting all of their worldly possessions on the line for success in any number of arenas. In this manner, a vast opening, a kind of emptiness is created that can attract what is most important to us. Following our path, we must release everything that stands between us and our greatness. Through physical detachment we realize that none of it really matters, that our physical reality is merely a reflection of all that we oppose and all that we attract from within ourselves.

⟫ Remember, we are merely spiritual beings within this vast physical experience, and attachment to anything other than our source is futile.

Amazing Life

This is it, our once in a lifetime opportunity!

. . . right here, right now, staring us right in the face.

What's holding us back? What's standing in our way?

There is so much to be grateful for and is so much to see.

Make the choice and everything will work out . . . in the end it always does.

Choosing Life

---●◆●---

Everything is something you decide to do,
and there is nothing you have to do.
—Denis Waitley

~ Did we choose to be here? If we chose to be here, can we leave? If we leave by choice, is there a penalty?

~ If we choose to stay, can we take full responsibility for the decision?

~ Do we reflect inward often enough? Do we understand why we are here, and are we all doing our part?

~ Can one person really change the world?

CHOOSING LIFE SURELY DOESN'T MEAN THAT WE WILL ALWAYS be happy with the consequences or the surrounding realities. Nobody said that we would receive everything we desired without effort, but by the nature of the commitment or contract to which we agreed, we have come to share and contribute in a manner that results in the betterment of all humankind. It almost seems impossible, or at the very least implausible, to make a personal contribution that has a lasting global impact, especially when the world looks as if it is at an all time low. There is civil unrest, poverty, disparity between the wealthy and the poor, destruction of the environment, threats of nuclear war, terrorism, oppression, overcrowding, and most importantly, a lack of faith and belief in the greater good of humankind and in ourselves.

> ~ At one point or another, we all chose to be here on this planet, but just because we chose to be here at one time does not imply that we are happy to be here now, nor does it presume in any way that life was meant to be easy.

Is our perspective on the world today any different than in generations past? There are equal amounts of great and wonderful things in this world visible to those who choose to see them, who choose not to be blinded by negativity. As a community, we have the opportunity to increase our awareness and connection to others and to our source such that we are able to see and appreciate more of what surrounds us. There is much to be said for seeing what we choose to see in the world, but what is more important is seeing where we can contribute and doing it.

> ~ If we choose to focus our energy on the problems or negativity of our world, there is no limit to the amount of negativity we will find.

We can all hope and pray for world peace or any other worthy desire; however, hoping or praying for something on a global scale has the tendency to leave us feeling powerless and helpless. In reality, we all have a very specific contribution to make, but it requires action as much as it requires the belief that positive change is possible, even if we cannot always see or experience the results of our efforts. Regardless of whether we perceive the world as large or small, segmented or cohesive, it operates on the contributions of many, just as a motorized vehicle or airplane requires the synchronization of thousands of moving parts.

⥽ We may not be able to change the world overnight, but by developing ourselves and doing our part in our families and our communities, whenever and wherever the opportunities present themselves, we will change the world one miraculous moment at a time.

We can affect global change by starting in our own backyard with our families and in our communities. We may underestimate the impact we make in every moment, but we cannot undervalue the power of our contributions over a lifetime. When global adaptation occurs, it is rarely the parting of the Red Sea moment we have all been enamored by. The intricacies and subtleties of global paradigm shifts can rarely be perceived or felt in the moment that they transpire. Actually, they occur over the course of our lifetime and the many to follow.

⥽ We must have faith and trust that through living our own greatness and staying true to our path and purpose in life, we will do our part to make our world everything it is destined to be, and more.

Carrying the World

Men go abroad to wonder
at the heights of mountains,
at the huge waves of the sea,
at the long courses of the rivers,
at the vast compass of the ocean,
at the circular motions of the stars,
and they pass by themselves without wondering.
—St. Augustine

➤ Why do we try to carry everyone else's problems on our shoulders?

➤ Why do we often feel responsible for other people's pain and suffering when we have more than we can handle with our own?

➤ Is our own struggle self-inflicted?

ALTHOUGH BEING OF SERVICE IS THE NOBLEST STATE OF BEING in this lifetime, it need not come at the sacrifice of ourselves, nor in the form of our often feeble and unachievable quest to fulfill another's path.

⤳ We cannot carry anyone except ourselves through this world.

We often feel the weight of the world on our shoulders, as if the evolution of the entire world were wholly dependent upon our individual actions and reactions. We often feel that the possibility of failure or the potential for success of those around us are aspects of our personal reality and consequences of our own actions. We feel responsible for ourselves and for our children, parents, friends, peers, and others with whom we may come in contact. We look at the world at large and wonder if we could do more, be more, and impact those around us in a greater way. Such is the ever-present inherent good within each of us. We move through life on a moment-by-moment basis, carrying everyone else's baggage, commitments and responsibilities that are not our own, yet have somehow became part of our responsibility.

⤳ Ultimately, we cannot be responsible for anyone other than ourselves just as we cannot control the actions of anyone else.

We have our own cross to bear, our own issues and baggage from this life and perhaps from those before it. We were not given the power to control others, but somehow we feel accountable for what can be judged as their success or failure. We think that we are responsible that they learn the lessons presented before them and make the "right" decisions. We waste precious energy and emotion caught up in the livelihood of others. We neglect the truth within ourselves and the focus to become present and honest so that we can evolve in this lifetime. Instead of serving others, we enable them to live lesser lives and sacrifice our own in the process.

⤳ We can serve others without taking on their pain. We can give to others without absorbing their suffering.

We can be the greatness we all believe is possible. But we must realize that, in the end, we are specifically accountable only for ourselves. We can raise our children and care for our parents, but in the end it is the choices we make individually that determine that quality of our existence. We must let go of everything beyond our control or we will break under the pressure and stress. Releasing others is not the same as becoming altruistic in our actions or beliefs; it is simply the liberation of any agenda so that we can be of service to those around us.

~ We cannot carry another's burden just as we cannot live another's life.

We must release others to walk their own path as we follow our own. The world allows for a life of service and commitment and provides the space for each of us to evolve at our own pace. By taking responsibility for ourselves, our actions, and our beliefs, we grant ourselves the freedom to provide selfless service, to give, and to allow others to become the greatness within themselves. If they choose not to evolve or not to accept the gifts we have to offer, we have lost nothing because we have nothing to lose.

~ We have everything to gain with a life of service, as it carries with it the potential for fulfillment, meaning, passion, and greatness.

Everything Works Out

━━━━◆━◆━━━━

Don't compromise yourself. You're all you've got.
—Janis Joplin

> ‍‍⁓ How much burden, worry, and stress do we carry around in
> our daily lives?
>
> ‍⁓ Why do we live life with such anxiety and distrust?
>
> ‍⁓ How is it possible for everything to work itself out over time?

IT TAKES A LOT OF STRENGTH TO CARRY THE WEIGHT OF THE
world all by ourselves. Life is often overwhelmed with concerns
about love, finance, family, relationships, and the track of society. We
make trite decisions about how to dress, what to eat, and where to
go; we also intermingle inquiries onto our path, especially when faced
with obstacles that test our core values and our very belief system. The
consistent theme, though, throughout all of life and all of existence is
that in the end, everything always works out—it *always* does.

⁓ It may take time, but in due course, we will discover and understand the meaning in all things.

History is filled with both glory and tragedy, but ultimately, conflict has a tendency to bring people together on a number of different levels. People have survived the most unbelievable tragedies, evolving to embrace an even greater level of connection, evolution, and even happiness. When things don't work out in life, we have full control over how we react to each challenge. We can choose to become upset, depressed, and even vengeful, but these reactions do not support our efforts to obtain what we truly desire. If something in our life doesn't work out the way we intended, perhaps there is something even better on the horizon. Of course in times of need or pain, this vision can be temporarily impaired, limited to the space within our reach, thus limiting our periphery.

~ How we choose to accept or reject our surrounding experiences determines the pain or pleasure we experience.

In the end, all of our responsibilities and requirements, demands and tasks, bills to pay, phone calls to make, and errands to complete really don't matter. The list is never-ending, as if meaningless duties somehow provide meaning in our life. We will all progress beyond this world, but we bring nothing with us, and we leave nothing behind save for memories. Hopefully, we will die a peaceful death when the time comes for us to move on. Our physical death will happen without a doubt, without our control, quite often without notice, and sometimes without even the slightest nuance of preparation. Death is something on which we can rely, expect, and accept.

~ Death is the inevitable outcome of life; it is the *only* thing we can be sure of. Our bodies will all decease, and then nothing matters except what we have given.

The universal energy around us moves everything forward as it is destined. We stress out, freak out, and elicit emotional and physical breakdowns as we try to control those experiences and moments that are essentially outside of our control. We cannot manage everything; in fact, we actually manage very little. We must let go of those situations, emotions, sensations, activities, experiences, and realities that elicit ongoing stress and pressure. As easily as we can choose which shoes to wear, we design our life and our experiences as a function of our choices and reactions to the world around us.

⁓ At the end of the day, we can all be assured that a new day will come, and the sun will rise again tomorrow.

The repercussions of yesterday become but a figment of our imagination as we recreate ourselves on a moment-by-moment basis. We are all given the gift of free will with the choices we make, who we desire to be, and how we choose to act in the process. The end is inevitable, but every evening most of us are granted the respite necessary to start over, to recreate our existence anew.

Remarkable Life

———◆◇◆———

Every man is his own ancestor, and every man his own heir.
He devises his own future, and he inherits his own past.
—H.F. Hedge

~ Why is it so difficult to find authentic peace and happiness?

~ Why do we struggle to locate the magnificence in everything, everyone, and every moment?

~ Why can life be so spectacular and amazing in one moment, yet in the next we are overwhelmed and challenged to see life for what it truly is?

WE LIVE OUR LIVES IN AN ATTEMPT TO DISCOVER PEACE AND happiness. With the trials of a life frequently surrounded by negativity, challenge, and temptation, these elements can be difficult to uncover. Life may be burdened by disappointment, frustration, and even death, but it is also enveloped with love, peace, happiness, and the excitement of adventure.

~ Each and every one of us has the opportunity to begin anew every day and in every moment.

As we live from moment-to-moment, not only do we realize how short life really is, but we have the opportunity to fully appreciate the gifts of both life and death. An action with a clear beginning and ending carries an urgency and permanence that urges us to grant it greater significance. A life with an end in sight makes time more valuable than it would be if the end were unclear. The concept of death can force us to overcome our weak and petty natures in order to become the fullness of ourselves in life, love, and happiness—as long as we don't cling to life as a result, paradoxically preventing us from truly living.

Do we really understand what life is all about, what it really means, or why we are here? The answers are uniquely different for each of us and can only be discovered by and through ourselves. Our experiences in this lifetime are a direct reflection of the results we attempt to achieve, and the meaning we place upon every experience. We are given the power of reason to consciously choose and experience a life as magnificent or traumatic as we can imagine. We are the captain of our own ship, and its destination or demise is ours alone.

~ We must consciously choose greatness in every moment, even when we are challenged with the greatest of life's lessons.

We are surrounded by splendor and magnificence during even seemingly insignificant moments. When we are present to and acknowledge the beauty in every moment, we have the opportunity to truly feel and share gratitude and peace in direct reflection of what we experience within ourselves.

Choose Now!

————◆◆————

We are made wise not by the recollection of our past,
but by the responsibility for our future.
—George Bernard Shaw

➤ What are we doing? What are we waiting for?

➤ Can we see that our life is passing us by?

➤ If we won't listen to our truth and follow our path, who will?

THERE ARE NO COINCIDENCES IN THIS UNIVERSE; EVERYTHING operates in perfect equilibrium. When we are ready, the right opportunities in life present themselves, whether in the form of people or things; and regardless of whether we see, hear, feel, or read it, it will speak to us. Irrespective of whether we agree or disagree with information as it is presented to us in life, it serves an important purpose to help us open our eyes to the world around us, to continually question what we believe, and to subsequently look within for the answers we seek for our truth.

⁓ The general complacency with which we live our lives offers little in the way of growth and evolution.

A healthy curiosity makes the world go around. We need to connect with others, step out of our comfort zone and out of our shell to become active participants in our communities. We need to engage in our world, express interest in other people's lives, be authentic, ask questions, and most importantly, learn from those around us. Everyone has a story, and there is something we can take away from every person we meet, from every connection we make, from every moment we live. Experiences happen as they are meant to, rarely as we expect them to. There are no accidents; and when a delay or inconvenience arises, remember that we are exactly where we need to be, in a position to connect and reconnect with those around us and our world at large. So, learn something new. Be of service. Evolve. Life is not all that mysterious; we just aren't able to plan out every moment of our lives as it will occur, regardless of our schedule or agenda, with or without our consent.

⁓ We can only plan out this moment; it really is the only one that matters.

We can take responsibility for this very moment and anything that transpires as a result of the divine plan of our life. Life is happens to us when we are not caught up in the planning of this moment or the one that follows. Life is what occurs when we let go of our agenda and become present to this moment. We need to gift ourselves the magnificence of the moment before us, a real present, the only present that truly exists.

⁓ There is a perfect time for all things, and *now* is that time.

It wasn't yesterday, for we were not ready. It is not tomorrow, for that will be too late. Now is the time for our own transformation, to make decisions for the betterment of our lives, our family, and our community. Now is the time to commit to our own evolution, to choose life over death, passion over complacency, greatness over mediocrity, service over selfishness. Now is the time to be the person we have always longed to be.

✤ We are irreplaceable so let us not waste this incredible opportunity.

In the end, what do we have to lose? Life is too short for anything less. We can study, read books, and plan out our lives, but in the end we must simply take action, climb that mountain, and dive into the ocean. The world awaits our unique contribution. This is the time, our time. We can make our world a better place, not by obsessing about what we did right or what we did wrong, but by helping to make every moment just a little bit better, a little more connected to our source, and a little more focused on a life of service.

✤ We are all destined for greatness. It is our choice alone whether we achieve all that is destined for us in this life.

We can choose to subsist through life, accepting everything as it is presented to us, or we can take advantage of the greatest opportunity before us—to become our true self, to follow our life-path, and to live a life of meaning and purpose.

Conclusion

There are no facts, only interpretations.
—Friedrich Nietzsche

IN THE END, IT IS THE QUALITY OF OUR LIFE AND NOT THE quantity. There will always be exceptions to every rule, each recommendation, and every aspect of humankind because we are imperfect creatures living in an imperfect world, thus creating the perfection we call life. We each have the opportunity to control our lives within the boundaries we are given; our happiness is in direct relation to our belief system, which in turn, is the basis for the choices we make and the feelings we experience in every moment. We cannot blame our unhappiness on anyone other than ourselves. Our conclusions, connections, and the entire reality of our existence are controlled by the conscious or unconscious choices we make in every moment.

~ We have the right to be happy and deserve to be—but we must choose it and we must earn it.

We need to give ourselves more credit for being a part of this world and for continuously giving all of ourselves to it. We deserve the fulfillment of our dreams. We merely need to remember the simple guidelines of the life we lead, and in time all of our dreams can be granted.

~ Appreciate every moment; continually let go, and trust that everything will work out.

~ Take responsibility for the choices you make without being too hard on yourself—accept yourself just the way you are.

~ Keep life simple; always look for harmony and happiness in all things where possible.

~ While focused on your own evolution, make new resolutions as often as possible, for it is positive and supportive of your purpose and passion in life. Then stick with it, at least in this moment, for your life deserves nothing less.

~ Practice unconditional love and see your world without prejudice or judgment.

~ Find balance in your financial affairs; practice financial wellness and always look for the beauty and spirituality in all things.

~ Learn not to take life too seriously; for none of us know how much time we have left. Stay positive, smile, and always be kind. We can always do what is right in our heart.

~ In this moment, appreciate the beauty in all things and all people while living life in moderation and balance.

~ As active participants in this world, realize that some are beyond repair and that we will never be able to please everyone.

~ Express kindness to those around you while seeking deep and fulfilling connection.

~ As part of your life-destiny, in every moment seek the answers to life's deepest questions, and in so doing, trust in your own greatness and that of the world around you.

➤ Most importantly, discover your truth in order to follow your path and purpose in life—in this moment and in every moment to come, without delay or restriction.

Last, but certainly not least, we cannot give up on human nature. Although we face skepticism and doubt, distrust and disease around many corners, we must not give up on the potential and greatness of each and every one of us to stay true to our path and purpose. We must do our part to make this world everything it is destined to be, and more.

➤ We are all born equal; we all maintain the *potential* for greatness, but not the requirement.

We all have the potential for excellence in our blood and in our soul, but it is not a mandate: it is optional, a choice that must be made again and again in every moment throughout our lives. We can choose to be the person we were yesterday, or we can choose to reinvent ourselves in this very moment and in every one that follows.

➤ Staying true to our path and purpose in life is more than a commitment; it is a lifetime of action.

Around every turn we are tested and pushed, questioned and released, continually given the opportunity to make the right decision, to grow and to become the greatness within ourselves. Inside this every moment and every one that follows, we have been given the responsibility and the power to choose, and that is the greatest freedom in this world. Life really is so very simple at its core. All challenges, cycles, and realities are easily reduced to a simple understanding of the sequences within humanity. How we live and what we do are all elements of the life we have chosen, that we continue to choose every moment of every day. The past and the future exist only within our mind, for this moment, the present moment is the only one that exists.

⤳ We must take responsibility for our choices and consciously choose life, greatness, and a path of excellence; it is the only destiny worthy of who we are.

About the Author

To thine own self be true.
—Shakespeare

INSTEAD OF USING THIS SECTION OF THE BOOK TO SHARE MY history, to showcase areas where I might proclaim my separateness or perceived authority or pre-eminence, I have chosen to use this section to share not how we are dissimilar, but how we are alike, for I am like you in more ways than you can imagine. In the end, every experience has granted me the opportunity to grow, learn, and evolve emotionally, mentally, physically and spiritually. These triumphs eventually became the fodder for every lesson detailed herein.

~ Who I have become in the process of experiencing and writing this book is far more important than the accolades, degrees and honors I have received, and more significant than anything I have acquired.

Your wisdom is not in direct proportion to the years of life lived, the number of books you have read, or the number of initials after your name. Wisdom is determined by your ability to assimilate and apply the guidance you receive toward the betterment of your life and in service to those around you. It is the quality, not the quantity of your life.

ᕙ This book is not the end result of my path, but the insights, wisdom, and clarity I discovered along the way.

I struggle like you, constantly searching for the right path and for the strength to overcome the moments of challenge and the ongoing opportunities for growth. In my own way, I suffer from the same pains, hopes, dreams, and fears that you do. Of my own manner, I follow the same path of truth and search for purpose, meaning, and evolution. I take care of myself, and as part of my path, I am of service to my family, my community, and our world at large. I seek connection in life in addition to balance and flow, just as you do. I pray for a world free of the ills that plague us, just as you do. I seek a world of peace, kindness, and happiness. I love just as you do, yet I struggle with the painful reality of our world, often making decisions in seclusion or separate from spirit or God, such that we tend to manifest the opposite of what we desire for ourselves.

ᕙ There is nothing in this book that you haven't heard or don't inherently know. The right path is only for our own choosing; it can only be determined by us, not for us.

We have a long way to go, individually and collectively, to achieve that which we believe is our destiny: to create a world that is better for our families, our children, and society itself. We are far from creating an appropriate level of communication, interconnectedness, and community that fosters love, caring, and support. The possibilities and opportunities are endless, and as we consciously create realities that support our belief systems, we will find what we seek and desire. We will discover a world where our community is the sacred whole, where we give merely for the happiness and fulfillment we receive, where we live to make the world a better place, and where in every moment and in every connection, we make a positive contribution to our greater world.

ᕙ We will find our home wherever we are, but only when we accept the fullness and greatness within ourselves and each other.

Afterword—The Awakening of Time

T HE MELTING SNOW DRIPS CARELESSLY FROM THE TOWERING world above, creating ever-expanding circles on the surface of the distilled pond, silent and patient. The world almost stops for this little moment in time, as if in appreciation of the seasons yet to come, reaping causality and a conscious and heart-felt instant of peace. We stop, virgin to the subtle consistencies of patience and in-the-moment appreciation. We breathe deeply the sensation of duality, that it might penetrate the darkness of our soul. We hold our breath, taking this meditative offering of our Earth Mother and soul along with us in our hectic day-to-day lives.

~ The world never stops and seems to continue in perpetuity, but in reality, our world will stop whenever we choose to be fully present with the moment before us.

The snow cowers under the pressure of the sun and falls carelessly down to the earth below. We are grateful for this moment in time, as if our entire lives have transpired to bring about this gratuitous breath of energy to support the coming day. Perhaps we will remember this sensation when we are challenged in life, working to fulfill our goals of financial abundance, success, true happiness, and fulfillment, or in service and dedication to our families. Perhaps we will envision the circulation of evolving charades as we reconvene within this world of technology to create our future. Perhaps we can be at peace wherever we are, connected to our inner world as much as we are present to our outer world.

If only for a moment, we realize that the world can go on without us. If we stayed in this moment forever, would we be fulfilled with gratitude or peace of mind? Would our inner hunger for life and love be satisfied by this momentary abundance of a world frozen in time? If the world were to end today, or merely our part in it, would anything really change?

We have read many stories of the men and women who came before us and relinquished the path we now seek to conquer. They were no different than we. They stood in query of their lives, feeling the same confusion and wonder that we do. We are not only lifetimes apart from them with respect to time, but also in terms of the inconsistencies between the life we have chosen and the lives they lived.

᠈⟍ The externality of our physical world is disconnected enough from our inner soul, yet deep within us lies dormant an entire world awaiting our discovery simply by connecting to our deep-seated inner passion.

Every morning we rise, and out of habit and circumstance, we recreate the momentary sensations of daily awakening. Are we strong enough to determine for ourselves the paths of consistent greatness and joy? If this is the case, why do strife and the grueling search for excellence abound? Are we the only ones conscious of our eternal patterning, as if the hardships of the path we walk throughout this lifetime were meant to fulfill even the most advanced among us? We are unique in the areas known and unknown to our sovereign intellect, yet we stand before thee as brother, sister, friend, and compatriot, dependent upon the existential, continuous, and eternal role of creation within us all.

⁓ We breathe in time under the assumption that time will give breathe to us, yet again.

We must learn from those before us in order to recall key lessons and understandings from previous lifetimes. Our time is very precious, and we must make the most of every moment, no matter how casual or insignificant it may seem. We often learn from others through observation and acceptance, for we have neither the time nor the energy to experience every lesson through our own volition. Some learning is best absorbed from afar, while other matters require the full integration of our being in order for us to evolve as we are destined.

We need peace of mind, if even momentarily, as we suffer the exhaustion wrought from our attempt to overachieve, as we work to fulfill our purpose in life and other crucial aspects of living for the eternal seeker within.

⁓ The lessons we live to experience—those of hope, passion, love, success, and fulfillment—create the moment we call life.

Acknowledgements

Don't compromise yourself. You're all you've got.
—Janis Joplin

H OW CAN ONE EVEN BEGIN TO ACKNOWLEDGE ALL OF THOSE who have touched our lives, who have played a role in our creation, in our refinement, in helping to shape us? We are the sum total of every opportunity, every decision, and every experience that has occurred thus far in our lives. Whether from those we love, those we hate, or even those we have never met, we have been shaped and formed by an infinite amount of input from all over the world, past and present, much of which we may have no conscious realization.

~ We receive in ways impossible to fully comprehend, just as we give and serve where the end contribution is rarely seen nor fully understood.

Our opportunity is to acknowledge the endless contributions we receive in so many ways throughout all of our lives, and to continue our commitment to improve not just the lives of those we love, but of our greater communities as well. We are forced to acknowledge every aspect of our world and community at large, such that those we love are given equal credence to those we hate, even though we are ashamed to admit it. Those who hurt us the most, who have caused us unimaginable amounts of pain, suffering, and grief are many times the most significant contributors to our evolution, for they help to shape and define who we are and help us fully commit to our path and purpose in life.

There is an intricate balance, not only in our outside world but also internally, as we pay tribute to all of the centers of our being. We acknowledge all aspects of ourselves, our day-to-day involvements and commitments to act responsibly as working adults, parents, good friends, heads of households, and contributing members of our societies. Outside of the world itself, we acknowledge those closest to our hearts on a moment-by-moment basis, whether our family, our friends, spirit, or our faith, belief, or divine path, that provide all the input and guidance we require and desire. With divinity and judgment aside, all of the actors deserve their credit for the roles they play in guiding and helping us to see, learn, understand, evolve on a continual basis, and to become the greatness to which each of us has been destined.

Thank you.,

Affirmation of Purpose

━━━━━━━━◆◆━━━━━━━━

FEAR NOT, DEAR SOUL, FOR YOUR WORRIES AND CONCERNS ARE not required. All preparations and reparations have preceded you; your physical body and spiritual presence is all that is required for the pace of humankind to progress into the greatness of time and the peace of timelessness. Breathe free and embrace your sovereign soul through the heart of the universe while surpassing the intellect, for it is the heart that holds the key to the power within. Grow to the fullness of yourself and consciously determine your reality from the truth within, beyond the whims and passing of hope and desire. Follow your mind to where you follow your heart; create balance in reason, for your destiny is created before your very eyes. Step firmly, or the earth beneath your feet will crumble for lack of intention, purpose, and structure. The motion of progression is the action of a conscious reality, created in the moment, of the moment, and for the moment.

Live free, for your freedom is the delimiter for which you search. Step into the night, for when the sun sets it will call upon you for service of the deepest intention. Be assured that it will call upon your mind, your heart, and your soul as it continues to rise and fall. Take responsibility for the manifest destiny before you, and accept the life of service before you, for it is why you are here.

All that you seek and all that you desire are here and ever present, simply for your choosing.

Highlights

- Money has the potential to destroy lives, incite war, and distract us from what is most important in life..

- We cannot sacrifice our life and soul in one area of our existence in an attempt to redeem ourselves in another.

- The general complacency with which we live our lives offers little in the way of growth and evolution.

- Often we are unable to let go of where we are in order to step forward on the path to greatness.

- Happiness, fulfillment, and connection are the true prosperity of the soul.

- We are poor not due to our lack of possessions, but due to our lack of appreciation and fulfillment in any particular moment.

- We need to be wealthy in our giving to others and caring for ourselves. We need to be rich in our personal evolution and growth.

- We cannot obtain happiness; we can only *be* happy. We cannot obtain love; we can only *be* loving.

- We are all born equal; we all maintain the potential for greatness, but not the requirement.

- Every moment is an opportunity for greatness, to make the changes that will bring us greater happiness and fulfillment.

- There is no coincidence to the life-path we have chosen.

- We can all benefit from the humbleness of a life of service and an openness to learn.

- We must learn to accept that everything happens as it is meant to, thereby allowing us to move confidently in the direction of our dreams.

- Spirituality freedom is making the choices in life that bring us true happiness and fulfillment.

- Living a life of balance is a constant, moment-by-moment integration of life's inner and outer priorities.

- We sacrifice for the wrong reasons and for the wrong people, often seeking financial abundance at the sacrifice of our spirituality, our health, and our quality time with our family.

- We have the right to be happy and deserve to be—but we must choose it and we must earn it.

- We are unable to find balance outside of ourselves.

- We use others as the benchmark for a balanced and healthy lifestyle, and by looking outside ourselves, we will always find what we are lacking in our own life.

- Happiness is all we can hope for; it is the most important aspect of our reality and the outcome of any successful experience.

- We cannot carry another's burden just as we cannot live another's life.

- In the end, it is the quality of our life and not the quantity.